T0098344

SPINOZA ON STATE AND RELIGION,

JUDAISM AND CHRISTIANITY

Also Available from Shalem Press:

The Hebrew Republic
Petrus Cunaeus

Political Hebraism: Judaic Sources in Early Modern Political Thought
Gordon Schochet, Fania Oz-Salzberger, Meirav Jones, editors

The Hebrew Republic
Carlo Sigonio

Forthcoming:

The Councils and the Judicial System Among the Ancient Hebrews
John Selden

The Law of Nature and of Nations:
According to the Teachings of the Hebrews
John Selden

SPINOZA ON STATE & RELIGION, JUDAISM & CHRISTIANITY

Hermann Cohen

Translated and with an Introduction by
Robert S. Schine

SHALEM PRESS
JERUSALEM

Shalem Press, 3 Ha'askan Street, Jerusalem
Copyright © 2014 by the Shalem Press

All rights reserved. No part of this publication may be reproduced, stored in
a retrieval system, or transmitted in any form or by any means, electronic,
mechanical, photocopying, or otherwise, without the prior permission of the
publisher, except in the case of brief quotations embodied in critical articles or
reviews.

Cover design: Erica Halivni

ISBN 978-965-7052-57-0

Printed in Israel

CONTENTS

INTRODUCTION

WHEN HERMANN COHEN arrived in Berlin in the autumn of 1912, the seventy-year-old professor of philosophy had just retired from his chair at the University of Marburg, where he had established what came to be known even in his lifetime as the Marburg school of neo-Kantianism. One of the very few Jews to hold a professorship in Germany—without forfeiting his faith at the baptismal font—Cohen had also become a cultural hero: From the prestigious perch of a university professorship he argued for the foundational role of the Jewish religion in the formation of the Western ideals of human dignity and social justice, and defended Judaism against the academic and intellectual elites who maligned it as an alien intrusion into the German nation. Though faced with anti-Jewish animus, Cohen held fast to his belief in a deep affinity—based on ideals—between the Jewish spirit and the German, a position that baffled both Judaism's detractors, to whom such an affinity seemed a risible fantasy, and Cohen's admirers, including his student Jakob Klatzkin, who conceded in a book he wrote as a philosophical eulogy to his teacher that Cohen's position on Judaism and "Germanism" revealed the tragic streak in his life and thought.[1] And in a 1968 letter Gershom Scholem diagnosed Cohen's belief in such a deep affinity as "totally fictive and unreal" from the start, a "utopian identification," and an example of the great "lie" of German Judaism. His letter continued:

> My father threw me out of the house in 1917 because I said: you and our family live in and through a lie. Cohen's position was probably the most noble and compelling form that this lie could assume, in a man of true moral greatness, but it was still just a lie, and that (even if it did not necessarily have to lead to the genocide of the Jews, something none of us imagined) was bound to lead somewhere.[2]

Elsewhere Scholem called Cohen the "unhappy lover" in the romance of the German-Jewish dialogue.[3]

So it is that reading Cohen demands a measure of historical sympathy, and a willingness to entertain his position and self-understanding as a German Jew. It requires philosophical sympathy, an inclination to accept, for the sake of a fair reading, the principles of the radical interpretation of Kant in the Marburg school, which endured long after Cohen's death as a force in the interwar years of the "crisis" of German thought.[4] Neo-Kantianism also motivated Cohen to designate Spinoza as the modern father of philosophical pantheism. However, in his final years Cohen's antipathy toward Spinoza went far beyond an aversion to pantheism. Spinoza became, in his eyes, the archenemy of Judaism and "the real accuser of Judaism in the eyes of the Christian world."[5]

Cohen's arrival in Berlin to teach at the Lehranstalt für die Wissenschaft des Judentums (Institute for the Scientific Study of Judaism) was cause for celebration. During his first semester he offered a lecture course and a seminar on Spinoza's *Theological-Political Treatise*. The annual report of the Lehranstalt conveys a sense of excitement: "The success of both the seminar and the lecture course matched their importance. The lecture hall of the Lehranstalt and the adjacent room could barely contain the size of the audience, which included people of all ages and social strata."[6]

One student who attended the seminar offers a more reserved assessment: the majority of the participants were unfamiliar with "Cohen's particular way of thinking or sensitivity." There was general consternation as it became evident that Cohen was using the seminar to gather material for a polemic against Spinoza. Furthermore, any gesture by those present to rally to Spinoza's defense was met with impassioned rebuttal. Cohen's monograph "Spinoza on State and Religion, Judaism and Christianity," published in 1915, is the product of that seminar held in Berlin in the winter of 1913. As noted by that student witness, historian Hans Liebeschütz, the monograph itself bears traces of its origins in a seminar room. One can almost hear Cohen speaking as he opens Spinoza's book, begins with the implications of the title, and proceeds to the text, "chapter by chapter."[7]

Cohen faults the title, *Theological-Political Treatise*, for omitting explicit mention of philosophy. He takes the book as a contrived and artificial combination of two discrete tractates addressing two topics that are connected not systematically, but only by the circumstances of Spinoza's life. The *Theological-Political Treatise* is, on the one hand, a *political* treatise in support of the liberalism of Spinoza's patron, Johan de Witt; and, on the other, it is a *theological* treatise in the sense that it is a critique of the Bible. It is intended to undermine the authority of the Bible, to demonstrate its human authorship—hence the significance of the book in the history of biblical criticism—and to show that it should in no way be considered of philosophical significance. According to Cohen, the first purpose can be attributed to Spinoza's close relationship to de Witt. The second purpose was to respond to his excommunication by the Jewish community of Amsterdam.

* * *

Hermann Cohen was born in 1842 in the small town of Coswig (Anhalt), where his father, Gerson, served as cantor and teacher, two functions often shouldered by one person in the smaller Jewish communities of Germany.[8] Hermann Cohen's wife, Martha, later recalled that the elder Cohen was devoted to his son's Jewish education, giving him his first Hebrew lessons at the age of three and a half, and continuing unabated when Cohen left home to attend the Gymnasium (secondary school) in nearby Dessau. Gerson Cohen would visit every Sunday, spending the entire day studying Jewish texts with his son.[9] At the age of fifteen, Cohen made what seemed a natural transition to the Jewish Theological Seminary in Breslau, and, as required by the curriculum, also studied at the university in the city. Recalling his teachers on the occasion of the jubilee of the seminary in 1904, Cohen wrote that its founder and rector, Zecharias Frankel, envisioned a rabbinate guided by science and scholarship. The German term and notion *Wissenschaft*, for which "science" alone is an inadequate translation, denoted the ideal of systematic knowledge grounded in methodologically consistent inquiry. "Genuine piety," Cohen wrote, characterizing Frankel's commitment, will "always be vitally engaged in scientific scholarship [Wissenschaft]." In Frankel's vision, the "Jewish community of the future" would not languish in literalist resistance to the idea of historical development but would welcome Wissenschaft as its guide and embrace the seminary's scholar-rabbis as teachers.[10] Cohen's particular conception of history as a moral struggle toward an infinite ideal shimmers through his recollection of Frankel here. One scholar has even argued that Cohen's very idea of an all-encompassing system of culture is indebted to the kind of system of Jewish learning he encountered at the seminary under Frankel's leadership.[11] In Cohen's scientific approach, Judaism as it should be is Judaism guided by "ideas."

These inclinations led Cohen to abandon his intention of becoming a rabbi, and he left Breslau to study philosophy in Berlin. He finally earned his doctorate at the University of Halle. His first published book, *Kant's Theory of Experience* (1871), caught the attention of Friedrich Albert Lange, a controversial social reformer who became professor at the University of Marburg in 1872 and arranged for Cohen's appointment as a lecturer there the following year. Cohen later reports on a conversation with his sponsor that occurred not long after his arrival in Marburg. When Lange asked him, "Do our views diverge on Christianity?" Cohen responded, "No, for what you call Christianity, I call prophetic Judaism." In Cohen's retelling, their shared "ethical socialism" bridged any religious differences, reflecting the essential harmony between Christian and Jewish ideals.[12] After Lange's death in 1875, Cohen succeeded him, becoming the first Jew to occupy a chair in philosophy at a German university. Franz

Rosenzweig attributes the government's approval of Cohen's appointment to a spell of liberalism in the early 1870s, a consequence of Bismarck's confrontation with the Catholic Church during the *Kulturkampf.*[13]

In Marburg, Cohen continued his reinterpretation of Kant but soon developed his own "system of philosophy," following the sequence of Kant's critiques—first epistemology, then ethics and aesthetics: *Logic of Pure Knowledge* in 1902, *Ethics of Pure Will* in 1904, and *Aesthetics of Pure Feeling* in 1912. Cohen gathered around him the circle of students that became known as the Marburg school of neo-Kantianism. Among them were those who remained close philosophical collaborators, such as Paul Natorp (1854-1924), and those who later parted ways, such as Ernst Cassirer (1874-1945), who turned to the philosophy of culture, and Jakob Klatzkin (1882-1948), who lamented Cohen's principled rejection of Zionism.

By the end of the 1870s, however, a wave of anti-Jewish animus swept through the German academic and intellectual world. The battle was joined when Heinrich von Treitschke, then the editor of the prestigious and nationalistic *Preußische Jahrbücher* (*Prussian Annuals*), published his infamous article "Our Prospects" in 1879. He wrote of the "multitudes of assiduous trouser-selling youths from the inexhaustible cradle of Poland, whose children and grandchildren are to be the future rulers of Germany's stock exchanges and Germany's press." In this article he penned the phrase that the National Socialists would later appropriate: "The Jews are our misfortune."[14] Cohen joined his former Breslau teachers, Manuel Joël, Heinrich Graetz, and others, in rebutting the attacks of the historian, in what came to be known as the "Berlin Anti-Semitism Controversy." Treitschke refused to publish Cohen's response in the *Prussian Annuals*, but Cohen published it elsewhere, in 1880, as his "Confession on the Jewish Question."

The essay opens with a sigh: "So once again it has come to this: we must confess our faith and loyalty."[15] Confronted with the German nationalist extrusion of Jews from German culture, Cohen never wavers in his faith in a deep, essential equivalence between German and Jewish ideals. He was convinced, as he had intimated to Lange, that the nation of Luther and the nation of the prophets were guided by the same moral principles. He was thus able to write in his "Confession" that Protestant Christianity and Israelite monotheism, when examined with respect to their "scientific" (*wissenschaftlich*)—read: "idealized"—concepts of religion, are indistinguishable. His conviction may seem fantastic to us now. In fact, as I write these lines, the copy of Cohen's *Jewish Writings* belonging to the National Library of Israel in Jerusalem lies open before me. In the margin, a startled reader penciled in a long series of oversized question marks. As Emil Fackenheim remarked on the fiftieth anniversary of Cohen's death, "Such was

Cohen's trust in both these worlds, in their inherent affinity, that he had no inkling or premonition that disaster was imminent."[16] To Cohen, meanwhile, the defense of Judaism in the German forum of ideas was a matter of national Jewish honor: confronted by Treitschke's charge that the Jewish nation is an interloper, Cohen found himself in "the most awkward personal position." Treitschke claimed that, because Judaism is the national religion of an alien people, Jewish monotheism is incompatible with the "messianic-humanistic idea" of a pure Christianity.[17] Treitschke's diagnosis challenges the very legitimacy of Cohen's own identity. He understood that he had accepted "the official obligation to instruct the youth of the academy on questions that are hardly indifferent with respect to religion," to defend German philosophy and ethics, and therefore to demonstrate to the Protestants who had entrusted him, a Jew, with this office that he was worthy of the mission of the German university. At the same time, Cohen never failed to rise to the defense of Judaism in the public square. He was therefore exceedingly sensitive to the responsibilities of the Jewish public intellectual: not merely to refrain from criticism of Judaism that would give succor to its detractors, but actively to defend its honor.

Introducing his monograph "Religion and Ethics" in 1907, Cohen concedes that there is slight prospect, in an intellectual atmosphere so universally hostile to Judaism, of initiating a serious, dispassionate discussion on topics of Jewish significance.[18] Yet he refuses to resign himself to what he calls "quietism" and to limit his role to that of an educator for his coreligionists alone, despairing of the power of "science [*Wissenschaft*] and philosophy." Rising above the animus of public opinion, he argues for the "significance of Judaism" with unerring faith in the power of scientific inquiry.[19] He would not waver in his conviction concerning the harmony, *in essence*, of German and Jewish ideals, even as he confronted their dissonance *in reality*. Rosenzweig reports that Cohen discontinued his regular course on Schiller, reluctant to expose his love of the poet and of the German spirit to the disrespect of a student audience that had become openly anti-Semitic.[20]

Nonetheless, in the summer of 1912, with Cohen's retirement from Marburg imminent, a group of students marched to his home in a "torchlight parade"—a *Fackelzug*—the highest form of appreciation German students could render to an admired professor. With an air of melancholy, Cohen addressed the assembly at his door: by the "glow of torches... you bring me comfort for many a worry, many a care, many an old injury, comfort that I will take with me from my official post into the privacy of my study."[21] Thus the founder of Marburg neo-Kantianism took his leave of Marburg for Berlin, where he focused on the nature of religion— he published his book *The Concept of Religion in the System of Philosophy* in

1915—and set to work on a philosophy of Judaism, *Religion of Reason out of the Sources of Judaism*. He was reviewing the galleys of that book when he died in 1918; it was published the following year. But Cohen's first project in Berlin was his reading of the *Theological-Political Treatise*.

* * *

The 1915 monograph was not Cohen's first statement on the *Theological-Political Treatise*. In 1910 he gave a lecture that was prompted, then as in 1915, by his objections to the Jewish veneration of Spinoza. The particular occasion was the naming of a new B'nai B'rith lodge in Berlin: "The Spinoza Lodge." In the 1910 lecture Cohen states that Spinoza's philosophical blasphemies fully justified his expulsion from the Jewish community.[22] But Cohen's efforts did little to slow the movement to reclaim Spinoza as a Jewish thinker and hero. Had Cohen lived longer, he would also have objected to the celebrations in 1927 of the 250th anniversary of Spinoza's death. At the ceremony at the Hebrew University in Jerusalem, historian Joseph Klausner declared the writ of excommunication null and void, invoking the old formula of rehabilitation, with great pathos and without any rabbinic authority to do so: "Our brother you are, our brother you are, our brother you are!"[23] Many years later, David Ben-Gurion wrote a lengthy essay on Spinoza titled "Let Us Make the Crooked Straight" for the newspaper *Davar* to do his own part toward Spinoza's rehabilitation.[24]

To be sure, German Jews probably venerated Spinoza in part because the modern liberalism from which they benefited had its foundation in his political theory. As Leo Strauss would write years later, "Prior to Hitler's rise to power most German Jews believed that their problem had been solved in principle by liberalism: German Jews were Germans of the Jewish faith, i.e., they were no less German than the Germans of the Christian faith or of no faith."[25] But Cohen makes only passing mention of the contribution of the *Theological-Political Treatise* to the founding of modern liberalism.[26] Rosenzweig, in fact, took him to task for his blindness to Spinoza's role in creating the very political conditions under which Cohen himself lived and thought.[27] Cohen was too preoccupied with Spinoza's merciless critique of Judaism, which he saw as one of the two main purposes of the *Theological-Political Treatise*.

Cohen's critique thus stems from both his fidelity to Judaism and his neo-Kantianism. The latter predisposed him to loathe Spinoza as the father of modern philosophical pantheism. But fidelity to Judaism animated Cohen's specific charges against Spinoza: one, that he deliberately eclipses the rationalist philosophical tradition in Judaism; and two, that he denies the essence of Judaism: the idea of ethical monotheism. Furthermore, Spinoza suppresses the facts: that Judaism introduced the idea of a universalistic human ethics into the history of civilization, that an idea of "natural religion"—the concept of the Noahide laws—is actually grounded in biblical thought and then developed and elaborated in rabbinic teaching.

* * *

Cohen's ethics are anchored in his Kantian foundations. As for Kant, so too for Cohen: ethics is conceivable only on the basis of the distinction between "what is" and "what ought to be." Just as in Cohen's theory of knowledge, where the structures of reason constitute the ideal toward which experience is directed, in ethics reason sets forth the ethical ideal toward which human action should strive. Cohen applies this principle across the spectrum of ethical and social endeavor.

Cohen and Kant differ significantly, however, on the relationship between ethics and religion. Kant was, so to speak, in the thrall of moral duty. Duty is the human reaction to unconditioned moral law, which Kant sometimes calls a "fact of reason." The *fact* of universally binding moral law *commands* our respect. It requires us, in turn, to concede that we must be capable of obeying it. Because we *ought* to do our duty, we *must* therefore be *free* to do it. Students reading Kant for the first time will often hear the formula "ought implies can": the fact of moral duty requires us to assume that human beings are free and thus able to act on their moral obligations. Kant establishes that freedom is a necessary assumption of ethics, in his terminology a "postulate." He proves not that the human will is free, but only that the assumption of a free will is a necessary "condition for the possibility" of ethics.

Kant presses this concept of the "postulate" further. Just as the "fact" of duty requires us to assume human freedom—using Kant's term, to "postulate" it—it also allows us to "postulate" the existence of God. As he sets out his argument in his late work *Religion Within the Limits of Reason Alone*, the idea of God is not ethically necessary, either to ground moral duty or as an incentive to fulfill it. Moral duty is an end in itself, requiring no external motive. The moral life does not promise happiness, for happiness is not the goal of ethics. Kant dismisses such conceptions of ethics as "eudaimonism." The moral life can be expected not to make one happy, but only worthy of happiness. Nevertheless, Kant posits the idea of a guarantor for the completion of moral progress, the idea of God. Kant thus accounts for the origin of religion as a concession to the human need to envision the consequences of one's actions. That is to say, although Kant's ethics is an ethics of conscience, concerned with motives, and although it is only the "good will," according to Kant, that can be called good without qualification, human beings are not indifferent to the results of their actions and seek assurance that their deeds will lead toward the realization of a just end. Human beings would like to see their own individual moral ends converging in a "kingdom of ends." Kant locates the origin of religion in this yearning for reassurance. Ethics has no need for religion, but human beings do. One can say, then, that the idea of God is not necessary to his ethics but is a "postulate" of "practical reason," of reason in action. Religion responds to a human metaphysical need that reason cannot satisfy with a philosophical proof. The "postulate" must suffice.[28]

For Cohen, however, the idea of God is a cornerstone of ethics. As early as 1872, in a letter explaining his early interpretation of Kant's ethics, Cohen writes: "It will seem odd to you that I have taken the Kantian God with me, but more than that, that I have arrived at the conviction that any attempt at an ethics is unconsidered and lacking in principle if it does not include such a God."[29] There is a methodological analogy in Cohen's neo-Kantianism between his logic and ethics. Just as the task of logic is to revise and refine the laws of scientific knowledge, the task of ethics is the moral improvement of humankind. Like the expansion and refinement of human knowledge, ethics is an infinite task. It teaches that there is always a gap between things as they are and things as they ought to be. The task of individuals is to use their freedom of will to strive for the ethical ideal. Philosophy, therefore, is not limited, as in Hegel's phrase, to "knowing" the world. It is not "absurd to fancy that a philosophy can transcend its contemporary world" or build "an ideal one as it ought to be."[30] Building a world as it ought to be is precisely the moral goal of human life. To Cohen, any philosophy that identifies the real with the ideal, thus effacing the distinction between "is" and "ought," is an invitation to Stoic quietism, leaving no place for the deployment of human will for the sake of the improvement of the world. In Steven Schwarzschild's words, "Hegelianism and socialist materialism, in short, are the denial of voluntarism in favor of quietism. Cohen is amazingly radical and consistent in the application of this criterion to all cultural and historical realities."[31] In his conviction concerning the capacity of free will to act in service of the social good, Cohen had also found an ally in his Marburg sponsor Friedrich Albert Lange.[32]

Cohen regarded the individual as the innermost of the concentric circles that constitute the moral world. A collective of individuals constitutes a state, and a collective of states constitutes a league of nations. These ethical structures are to be unified in the perfection of humankind. History *as it is* staggers on from one injustice, conflict, and war to another; history *as it ought to be* is a constant striving for this all-encompassing ideal. Ethics is the infinite task of laboring toward the realization of this ideal, toward a world of universal justice, toward the messianic age. Cohen's ethics of the ideal is immune to any refutation by facts. It is disproven by neither injustice nor genocide. It is an ethics of rational hope in a messianic future, guaranteed by God.

To Cohen, then, God is the guarantor of this ultimate unity; God is "the paradigm of morality." The God idea is therefore unique, and thus distinct from existence itself. If this distinction is blurred, between things as they are and things as they ought to be, pantheism is the result, mistaking the real for the ideal. Ethics is impossible. The philosophical collision with Spinoza was inevitable.

* * *

Now, it is true that in a very early anonymous essay on Heine, Cohen had suggested that pantheism and monotheism might be compatible. He claimed an intimate relationship between monotheism and "strictly philosophical pantheism."[33] In his mature work *Ethics of Pure Will* he even concedes that pantheism has the merit of overcoming personification by identifying God with the cosmos as a whole. The personification of God, in Cohen's view, always leads to mythology. However, his principled aversion to pantheism crystallized by 1904, and then remains consistent: pantheism renders ethics impossible because it identifies God and nature as one and the same. The true relationship between God and nature, however, is not "identity." Nature and God should be correlated, but not identical, and their relationship is that of a "harmonizing unity," in which the God idea guarantees the eventual harmony of the world and God, of natural existence and God, as the paradigm of morality.[34] The "oneness" of God, accordingly, does not indicate mere quantity—one God as opposed to many gods. It indicates the "uniqueness of God" as the moral ideal.[35] Any system that muddles this distinction between the real and the ideal is thus a form of pantheism, and annuls the possibility of ethics.

It is easy to see why Cohen would argue that Jewish monotheism represents the historical *origin* of philosophical ethics. He never tired of defending the significance of Judaism before the forum of philosophy and in the arena of German culture. It was a matter of both Jewish and philosophical honor.

This, then, is the basis of Cohen's main philosophical charge against Spinoza: he undermines the very possibility of ethics. Cohen cannot conceive of ethics except as based on the distinction between the real and the ideal. Spinoza's monistic equation of God and nature—*Deus sive natura*—erases that distinction, declaring that "what is" is also "what ought to be," that, as in Pope's verse, "whatever is, is right." Spinoza's ethics, likewise, does not allow for the idea of freedom: what human beings understand to be freedom is nothing but a flawed or incomplete conception of the causes of one's actions. Spinoza writes in the *Ethics*: "Their idea of freedom, therefore, is simply their ignorance of any cause for their actions."[36] His worldview is a thoroughgoing determinism: "In the mind there is no absolute or free will; but the mind is determined to wish this or that by a cause, which has also been determined by another cause, and this last by another cause, and so on to infinity."[37] In Spinoza's conception, freedom consists, paradoxically, in being conscious of the true causes of one's actions, and thus acting according to the guidance of reason. This idea of freedom, a reprise of a Stoic line of thinking, is irreconcilable with the Cohenian-Kantian idea, for freedom of the will consists precisely in the capacity of the human being for spontaneity.[38] To Cohen, the very title of Spinoza's magnum opus, the *Ethics*, is a misnomer. His sole contribution to an understanding of human action is his analysis of the emotions, which he observes as if they were lines and angles: it is mathematics of human feelings. To Cohen, however, ethics is not descriptive; it is normative, and an ethics without the assumption of human freedom is a contradiction in terms.

Cohen's general *philosophical* charge against Spinoza, then, seems to be based on a reading of Spinoza's *Ethics*, not the *Theological-Political Treatise*: in his *Ethics* Spinoza undermines the possibility of ethics and thereby degrades what it means to be human. Cohen's *specific* charges against Spinoza seem to have been motivated by his reading of the *Theological-Political Treatise*: that Spinoza deliberately and malevolently misrepresents Judaism.[39] For Cohen, ethical monotheism represents Judaism's historical contribution to human civilization. The prophets taught that God calls all humankind to the ideal of universal justice. Judaism is thus the historical source of universal ethics.[40] Spinoza, however, dismisses Judaism and its sources. The significance of the Bible, in his reading, is that it provided the constitution of the Jewish commonwealth. It was relevant for as long as a Jewish state existed, and was therefore, after the demise of the commonwealth in the year 70 c.e., consigned to irrelevance. Throughout the *Theological-Political Treatise*, Spinoza pursues a policy of "malicious reductionism."[41] He narrows his definition of religion to "obedience to God." Particularly offensive to Cohen is the consequence that religion has nothing to do with knowledge or rationality.

Furthermore, Cohen charges that Spinoza denies what, to Cohen, is a corollary of a universal ethics: the conception of a universal moral law, first articulated in the Bible as the commandments God gave to the descendants of Noah, the "Noahides." Since biblical history takes Noah as the progenitor of humankind, the Noahide commandments were binding on humanity and represent the first historical instantiation of the idea of universal moral law. Hence, the very idea of such law, even if it is also of timeless validity because it can be derived from reason, is the unique historical contribution of Judaism to civilization. Spinoza, in contrast, makes no mention of this foundational Jewish teaching. Worse yet, he "suppressed the concept of the *Noahide*," even though, in Cohen's estimation, "as a term in constitutional law it represents an astonishing manifestation of the universal idea of natural religion, in the form of *the fundamental idea of Jewish monotheism*"—the words with which Cohen closes the monograph, "Spinoza on State and Religion, Judaism and Christianity."[42] Spinoza's omission of this foundational idea can only have been a deliberate defamation of Judaism, and Cohen devotes much ink in his monograph to remedying Spinoza's distortion.

According to Cohen the distortion extends even to Spinoza's misreading of Maimonides' statements on the Noahide laws. At issue is the question of whether the Noahide must believe in the divine origin of these laws in order to "enjoy a share in the world to come." In short: is a moral life motivated by reason alone sufficient to earn divine reward, or must the moral life be motivated by belief in revelation? In a particularly impassioned critique, Cohen accuses Spinoza of selective quotation and misrepresentation: Spinoza intended to make Maimonides appear to have taught, in the famous passage in his *Commentary on the Mishna*, tractate Sanhedrin 10, that those who accept the fundamental laws of ethics—the Noahide laws—only because they are persuaded of their rationality are inferior to those who accept them as divine commandments. The latter have a share in "the world to come," while the former do not, nor are they to be regarded as "wise," that is, as philosophically astute. To be sure, Maimonides' position is not as clear-cut as Cohen would have his readers believe.[43] Whatever the merits of the philological case against Spinoza, Cohen charges him not only with misrepresenting Judaism, but also with willfully obscuring Maimonides' universalist rationalism.

Seeking a motive for the ferocity of this attack on Judaism, Cohen finds it in Spinoza's biography: the *Theological-Political Treatise* is his literary revenge on the Jewish community of Amsterdam, which excommunicated him in 1656. The *Treatise* slanders Judaism: Spinoza denies the universality of Judaism's ethics, he denies the ethical teachings of the prophets, and he disavows the Jewish rationalist philosophical tradition, declaring, against its foremost exponent, Maimonides, that the Bible and philosophical truth are incompatible. He ascribes the survival of the Jews not to fidelity to the Torah, but to the ritual of circumcision and to the hostility of other peoples—*odium nationum*—which steeled the Jewish will to endure. The Torah had only one purpose, to serve as the legal framework of a state. He reduces Judaism to secular politics. At the same time, he elevates Christianity to a position of superiority. To Cohen, Spinoza's *Theological-Political Treatise* amounts to a "*humanly incomprehensible betrayal.*"[44]

* * *

Cohen's anger is understandable; it springs from his own position as a Jew occupying a prestigious post in German society. He considered fidelity to one's nation a duty. A Jew should defend Judaism, and certainly not disparage it. Furthermore, to make the case—to offer an *apologia*—one had to possess clarity about the "proper relationship between religion and ethics." Such "clarity," in Cohen's view, meant recognizing the deep agreement between Jewish ethics and German humanism. When asked, for example, for his opinion of a candidate for a new professorship in philosophy of religion at the Berlin Hochschule, the Academy for the Science of Judaism, a chair that was to be named in his honor, he demurred on the grounds that he could not "entrust our philosophy of religion to anyone who has not achieved perfect clarity about the relationship of philosophy of religion to ethics."[45] Cohen took his own position as the representative of Judaism in the public square with the utmost seriousness; he bore responsibility for presenting a philosophical argument for Judaism before a German public. In his eyes Spinoza was a colleague and coreligionist who had not only failed in this responsibility but even acted contrary to it, in the only major work published during his lifetime. Spinoza's actions were morally reprehensible, a breach of *fidelity* to his inherited religion, even his nationality. Furthermore, Cohen complains that Spinoza's defamation of Judaism "came to be regarded as the confession of a crown witness who, by virtue of his philosophical genius and expertise in the field of Judaism, possessed unassailable authority."[46] Spinoza even misled Kant into construing Judaism as a religion of "statutory laws," a religion therefore of servitude, not freedom.[47] Cohen charges that Spinoza's legacy extends into his own day:

> That it is possible for anti-Semitism to celebrate its orgies in our age, at the same time as academic Protestant theology has produced illuminating studies leading to a new understanding of Israelite prophecy—this would be inexplicable were it not for the demonic spirit of Spinoza, still poisoning the atmosphere from within and from without. The pithy slogans that Spinoza employed to vent his vengeful hatred of the Jews can be found even now, almost verbatim, in the newspapers of those political camps.[48]

Readers of Cohen have attempted to map the route that led from his romantic reading of Spinoza in his youth to the polemical indignation of the 1915 monograph. There is little evidence of any probing engagement with the *Theological-Political Treatise* before the last decade of Cohen's life. Nor does it seem plausible that the ostensible late "turn" toward Judaism—a view made dominant by Rosenzweig's portrait of Cohen—was a factor in his polemical condemnation of Spinoza.[49] More plausible is the simpler explanation: that

Cohen, who already saw in Spinoza his great philosophical adversary, took genuine umbrage at Spinoza's assault on Judaism in the *Theological-Political Treatise*.

* * *

"Cohen took Spinoza seriously. For this reason, his Spinoza has not been taken seriously."[50] So notes Rosenzweig in his foreword to Cohen's posthumously published lecture on Spinoza from 1910. Blinded by their desire to claim Spinoza as one of their own, Jews on the whole preferred to ignore Cohen's challenge. The only thinker who did take Cohen's Spinoza seriously was the young Leo Strauss, in "Cohen's Analysis of Spinoza's Bible Science,"[51] a critique he published in 1924, the year Cohen's collected writings on Judaism were published, and the Spinoza monograph caught Strauss' eye. In that essay Strauss argues that Cohen, blinded in turn by his "apologetic interest," failed to see that the *Treatise* can be understood "without any reference to Spinoza's empirical connection to Judaism."[52] Cohen assumes that the *Theological-Political Treatise* represents Spinoza's literary revenge for his excommunication by the Amsterdam Jewish community.[53] Strauss, however, demonstrates that Spinoza's main object in the *Treatise* is to invalidate not Judaism, but revealed religion of any kind. He claims that Cohen failed to appreciate Spinoza's philosophical and political context. Strauss points out, for example, that it would have been superfluous, in the intellectual environs of the seventeenth century in which Spinoza was writing, to make explicit mention of "philosophy" in the title of the *Theological-Political Treatise*. It was understood, as it was for Hobbes' *Leviathan*, that philosophy is implicated in the "theological-political" problem. As a consequence, the *Treatise* is better understood as a chapter not in the history of Jewish thought, but in the history of the European Enlightenment.[54] Strauss later credited his reading of the Cohen essay with posing the question that occupied his political thought for a lifetime: the philosophical conflict between reason and revelation, between the Enlightenment and revealed religion, between "Jerusalem and Athens."

Cohen's confrontation with Spinoza is illuminated by seeing it in the light of the "Jewish question"—that term for the very presence of Jews in Germany before the question's "final" resolution. Cohen's solution, as we have seen, was to dismiss the question altogether by giving an account of Jewish identity that would establish a harmony between Jewish values and the values of German humanism in the Kantian tradition. The "Jewish question" found its answer in his demonstration that the "sources of Judaism" would reveal Judaism as a "religion of reason" when properly understood as stages in the career of humanity straining toward its ideal state. Cohen's "messianic age" is thus a Jewish analogue to Kant's "kingdom of ends." Cohen believed that Jewish messianism was the essence of Jewish teaching. Its goal of a united humankind assigned to Jews the task of laboring toward that messianic vision and of enduring whatever hardships or suffering their role in world history entailed. For this reason, in his posthumously published *Religion of Reason out of the Sources of Judaism*, he speaks, eerily now, of the "messianic sufferings of Israel." The "Jewish question" thus dissolves into a messianic future, made possible by the harmony of Jewish and humanistic moral ideals. Cohen's purported "solution" of the "Jewish question" is precisely what Scholem dismissed as "utopian."

It is obvious that Cohen's vision of the messianic future would lead him to reject Zionism, another possible answer to the "Jewish question," which was just beginning to gain a following, mainly among young German Jews. Zionism, he maintained, was a regressive move, forfeiting Judaism's world-historical mission for the sake of limiting its goal to the establishment of a particularistic, secular state. Cohen seems neither to recognize nor to anticipate that Spinoza's secularizing reduction of Judaism could and would be appropriated or invoked by Zionist thinkers. Cohen does report on Spinoza's strange speculation toward the end of chapter 3, "Election," in the *Theological-Political Treatise*. After explaining that the sign of circumcision has been, along with universal hatred of the Jews, the main reason for Jewish survival, Spinoza continues: "Indeed, were it not that the fundamental principles of their religion discourage manliness, I would not hesitate to believe that they will one day, given the opportunity—such is the mutability of human affairs—establish once more their independent state, and *that God will again choose them*." Cohen, taking Spinoza as seriously as ever, notes that this prediction contradicts the latter's view on divine providence—that is, he denies it—and writes the remark off to a "diabolical sense of irony."[55] It is curious that this proto-Zionist sentiment did not draw Cohen's ire; the thinkers of the Zionist movement he opposed had discerned here not irony, but support for Zionism as a force for secularization, reducing Judaism to a political entity.

During his lifetime, Cohen was attacked for his opposition to Zionism by Martin Buber, and Cohen construed the attack as a "thrust of the dagger" aimed at his entire philosophical system, at his relationship to reality.[56] With a certain pathos he defends his philosophical life work, arguing that Buber *must* know that for him the concept of "nature" is constituted by reason, as if this public dispute on Zionism could be cleared up by a mere reference to Cohen's system of critical idealism and by a reminder that he derives his concept of nature from pure logic, leaving no metaphysical residue. It is irrelevant, then, to invoke the "natural" as a quantity of any significance in a debate on culture. Buber in turn accuses Cohen of being too ethereal, a custodian of concepts who is blind to reality. Cohen responds that "reality" is the pure construction of transcendental logic. He has no objection to "nationality," and has even called for its cultivation, but only as something of ethical value for the realization of universal ethical norms.[57] Cohen has to object to the implication of Zionism that the purpose— the telos—of Jewish existence can be fulfilled in secular political reality. It therefore amounts to the elision of the distinction between the "real" and the "ideal" and is thus a lapse, in Cohen's terms, into pantheism. It was not just an offhand remark when Cohen allegedly said to Rosenzweig that the problem with Zionists was that "those fellows want to be happy!"[58] Zionism represented, to Cohen, a lapse into eudaimonism, the desire to be "happy," a moral mistake. It may be a "solution" to the Jewish problem, but it comes at the cost of Judaism, for it amounts to an apotheosis of the state.

It was Cohen's good fortune that he was spared the trauma of the annihilation of his "utopian" vision. His wife, Martha, was less fortunate and perished in the "model" concentration camp at Terezin-Theresienstadt on September 12, 1942.[59] Her death in the genocide of European Jewry represents a tragic, posthumous rebuke to Cohen's messianic hope. Yet the theoretical problem he addresses— what Leo Strauss would call the "theological-political" problem—remains: whether the foundations of the liberal state, in which freedom of thought must be guaranteed, demand as a price the forfeiture of religion. Spinoza's answer is clear. Cohen's is more complex: religion is sustainable in the liberal state if it renounces claims to political sovereignty, and that renunciation is possible only because he sees a perfect alignment between Judaism, as a religion of reason that emerges from its own sources, and the goals of the liberal state as a stage in the progress of humankind toward a messianic future. That is the more general significance of Cohen's conviction that there is a deep affinity between the ideals of German and Jewish culture, a historical idealism to which, we must presume, he would have adhered even in the face of the cruelest empirical facts. Though Cohen's convictions about the harmony of Jewish and German culture may now seem tragically quaint and naive, his moral seriousness may yet speak to this and future generations. In him we encounter a man of indomitable hope, who, as a Jew and a philosopher, was proud to defend the particular religion into which he was born, because he understood it as a religion of reason, as the source of the universal moral ideals in which all instruments of human striving—among them state and religion—must converge.

NOTES

1. Jakob Klatzkin, *Hermann Cohen* (Berlin: Jüdischer Verlag, 1919), p. 10.

2. Gershom Scholem to Karl Löwith, August 31, 1968, in Gershom Scholem, *Briefe*, vol. 2, *1948-1970*, ed. Thomas Sparr (Munich: C.H. Beck, 1995), p. 214. Löwith had sent Scholem the manuscript of his article "Philosophie der Vernunft und Religion der Offenbarung in H. Cohens Religionsphilosophie," which appeared in *Sitzungsberichte der Heidelberger Akademie der Wissenschaften, Philosophisch-historische Klasse* (Heidelberg, 1968). Scholem explains his dismissal of the "German-Jewish symbiosis" as a fiction in a number of essays, including "Against the Myth of the German-Jewish Dialogue" and "Once More: The German-Jewish Dialogue," in *On Jews and Judaism in Crisis: Selected Essays*, ed. Werner J. Dannhauser (New York: Schocken, 1976). All translations from the German are my own.

3. "Unhappy lover" appears in "Against the Myth," p. 63. Cohen's own interpretation of the relationship between *Deutschtum und Judentum* ("Germanness" and Judaism) is rooted in his philosophical system, as Hartwig Wiedebach has demonstrated in the most comprehensive and systematic study to date of Cohen's remarkable position: *Die Bedeutung der Nationalität für Hermann Cohen* (Hildesheim: Georg Olms Verlag, 1997), published in English as *The National Element in Hermann Cohen's Philosophy and Religion* (Leiden: Brill, 2012).

4. For an insightful and compact account of Marburg neo-Kantianism and its afterlife, see Peter Eli Gordon, *Rosenzweig and Heidegger: Between Judaism and German Philosophy* (Berkeley: University of California Press, 2003), pp. 39-81. Ulrich Sieg gives the full account in *Aufstieg und Niedergang des Marburger Neukantianismus* (Würzburg: Königshausen & Neumann, 1994).

5. See below, p. 58.

6. *Einunddreißigster Bericht der Lehranstalt für die Wissenschaft des Judentums* (Berlin, 1913), p. 6, cited by Hartwig Wiedebach in his introduction (*Einleitung*) to *Kleinere Schriften V, 1913-1915*, vol. 16 of Hermann Cohen, *Werke* (Hildesheim: Georg Olms Verlag, 1997), p. xvii. Wiedebach has reconstructed a list of all of Cohen's courses during the war years.

7. Hans Liebeschütz, "Hermann Cohen und Spinoza," *Bulletin für die Mitglieder des Leo Baeck Instituts* 12 (1960), p. 225.

8. Franz Rosenzweig's sweeping introduction to the 1924 edition of Cohen's *Jewish Writings* must be used with caution as a biographical source. Highly interpretive, Rosenzweig argues that Cohen's late thought was animated by a "return" to Judaism that brought on a break with his philosophical idealism. Even though Rosenzweig's reconstruction was convincingly refuted by Alexander Altmann in his 1962 essay "Hermann Cohens Begriff der Korrelation" (Hermann Cohen's Concept of Correlation), the former's thesis continued to dominate the reading of Cohen's late work. A. Altmann, "Hermann Cohens Begriff der Korrelation," in *In Zwei Welten: Siegfried Moses zum 75. Geburtstag* (Tel Aviv, 1962), reprinted in Altmann, *Von der mittelalterlichen zur modernen*

Aufklärung: Studien zur jüdischen Geistesgeschichte (Tübingen: J.C.B. Mohr [Paul Siebeck], 1987), pp. 300-317. Because personal anecdotes also figure in Rosenzweig's biography, Steven Schwarzschild's commentary is indispensable: "Franz Rosenzweig's Anecdotes About Hermann Cohen," in *Festgabe für die jüdische Gemeinde zu Berlin 25 Jahre nach dem Neubeginn*, ed. Herbert A. Strauss and Kurt R. Grossmann (Heidelberg: Lothar Stiehm Verlag, 1970), pp. 209-218. See also the critical commentary of Thomas Meyer, *Vom Ende der Emanzipation: Jüdische Philosophie und Theologie nach 1933* (Göttingen: Vandenhoek und Ruprecht, 2008), pp. 133f.

9.   Martha Cohen records her reminiscences in her foreword to *Religion der Vernunft aus den Quellen des Judentums* (Religion of Reason out of the Sources of Judaism), Cohen's final work, published posthumously in 1919. She was the daughter of Louis Lewandowski (1821-1894), the celebrated Berlin cantor and composer.

10.   Hermann Cohen, "Ein Gruß der Pietät an das Breslauer Seminar" (1904), in *Jüdische Schriften*, vol. 2, p. 423 (hereafter JS).

11.   See Dieter Adelmann, *"Reinige Dein Denken": Über den jüdischen Hintergrund der Philosophie von Hermann Cohen*, ed. Görge K. Hasselhoff (Würzburg: Königshausen & Neumann, 2010).

12.   Retold by Rosenzweig in his introduction ("Einleitung") to Cohen's *Jüdische Schriften*, JS 1:xxvf.

13.   Rosenzweig, "Einleitung," in *JS*, vol. 1, p. xxvi.

14.   Heinrich von Treitschke, "Our Prospects," excerpted in Marcel Stoetzler, *The State, the Nation, and the Jews: Liberalism and the Antisemitism Dispute in Bismarck's Germany* (Lincoln: University of Nebraska Press, 2009), pp. 309-316, esp. p. 312 and 314. Treitschke's article was originally published as "Unsere Aussichten" in *Preußische Jahrbücher* (November 1879), and reprinted in Walter Boehlich, ed., *Der Berliner Antisemitismusstreit* (Frankfurt a.M.: Insel, 1988), and again in the more exhaustive collection by Karsten Krieger, ed., *Der Berliner Antisemitismusstreit 1879-1881* (Munich: K.G. Saur, 2003). See also Michael A. Meyer, "Great Debate on Anti-Semitism: Jewish Reaction to New Hostility in Germany, 1879-1881," *Leo Baeck Institute Year Book* 11 (1966), pp. 137-170.

15.   "Ein Bekenntnis in der Judenfrage," in *JS*, vol. 2, pp. 73-94. Cohen writes: "Es ist also doch wieder dahin gekommen, daß wir uns bekennen müssen" (p. 73). Cohen uses vocabulary—*Bekenntnis* (confession) in the title and *sich bekennen* (to confess) in the first sentence—that may extend beyond the religious, as it does here.

16.   Emil Fackenheim, "Hermann Cohen After Fifty Years," LBI Memorial Lecture No. 12 (New York: Leo Baeck Institute, 1969), p. 4.

17.   Cohen, "Bekenntnis," *JS*, vol. 2, p. 74.

18.   Cohen, "Religion und Sittlichkeit," in *JS*, vol. 3, pp. 98-168.

19.   Cohen, "Religion und Sittlichkeit," in *JS*, vol. 3, p. 98.

20.   Rosenzweig, "Einleitung," in *JS*, vol. 1, p. xxxix.

21.   Hermann Cohen, "Rede anlässlich des am 25. Juli 1912 dargebrachten Fackelzuges," in *Hermann Cohens Schriften zur Philosophie und Zeitgeschichte*, ed. Albert Görland and Ernst Cassirer (Berlin: Akademie-Verlag, 1928), vol. 2, p. 471.

22.   Hermann Cohen, "Ein ungedruckter Vortrag Hermann Cohens über Spinozas Verhältnis zum Judentum," introduced by Franz Rosenzweig, in *Festgabe zum zehnjährigen Bestehen der Akademie für die Wissenschaft des Judentums 1919-1929* (Berlin: Akademie-Verlag, 1929), p. 59.

23.   "Ahinu ata, ahinu ata, ahinu ata!" Joseph Klausner (1874-1958) was a professor of literature at the Hebrew University. For an account of the Jerusalem ceremony (on p. 114) and a comprehensive history of the image of Spinoza in modern Jewish culture, see Daniel B. Schwartz, *The First Modern Jew: Spinoza and the History of an Image* (Princeton, N.J.: Princeton University Press, 2012).

24.   David Ben-Gurion, "*Netaken Hameuvat*" [an allusion to Ecclesiastes 1:15], *Davar*, December 25, 1953, p. 3.

25.   Preface to Leo Strauss, *Spinoza's Critique of Religion*, trans. E.M. Sinclair (New York: Schocken, 1965), p. 4.

26.   See below, p. 3.

27.   Introduction to "Ein ungedruckter Vortrag," p. 44.

28.   Kant gives his account of "postulates" of pure practical reason in the *Critique of Practical Reason* (1788), and his most succinct account of the origin of religion in the preface to the first edition of his late work *Religion Within the Boundaries of Mere Reason and Other Writings*, Cambridge Texts in the History of Philosophy, ed. Allen Wood and George di Giovanni (Cambridge: Cambridge University Press, 1998), pp. 33-36.

29.   "Merkwürdig wird es Dir sein, daß ich den kantischen Gott mitnehme, ja noch mehr, daß ich zu der Überzeugung gekommen bin, jeder Versuch in der Ethik sei gedankenlos, principlos, der ohne einen solchen Gott gemacht wird." Hermann Cohen, *Briefe*, ed. Bruno Strauß and Bertha Strauß (Berlin: Schocken-Verlag, 1939), p. 42.

30.   G.W.F. Hegel, *Philosophy of Right*, trans. T.M. Knox (Oxford: Clarendon Press, 1941), p. 11.

31.   See Steven Schwarzschild's fine and not uncritical essay "The Democratic Socialism of Hermann Cohen," *Hebrew Union College Annual* 27 (1956), pp. 417-438, esp. p. 424.

32.   For the political significance of neo-Kantianism, see Thomas E. Willey, *Back to Kant: The Revival of Kantianism in German Social and Historical Thought, 1860-1914* (Detroit: Wayne State University Press, 1978).

33.   Hermann Cohen, "Heinrich Heine und das Judentum," in *JS*, vol. 2, p. 9.

34.   Summarizing Hermann Cohen, *Ethik des reinen Willens* (Berlin: Ernst Cassirer, 1904), pp. 437-438.

35.　Hermann Cohen, *Religion of Reason out of the Sources of Judaism*, trans. Simon Kaplan (New York: Ungar, 1972), ch. 1, "God's Uniqueness."

36.　Spinoza, *Ethics*, book 4, proposition 35, note.

37.　Spinoza, *Ethics*, book 2, proposition 48.

38.　For the Stoic elements in Spinoza, see Paul Oskar Kristeller, "Stoic and Neoplatonic Sources of Spinoza's Ethics," *History of European Ideas* 5 (1984), pp. 1-15.

39.　Franz Nauen, "Hermann Cohen's Perceptions of Spinoza: A Reappraisal," *AJS Review* 4 (1979), pp. 111-124.

40.　Cohen sets forth his understanding of a historical "source" in the introduction to his *Religion of Reason*, pp. 24-30.

41.　The phrase is Steven Schwarzschild's, in "Do Noachites Have to Believe in Revelation? (A Passage in Dispute between Maimonides, Spinoza, Mendelssohn, and Hermann Cohen): A Contribution to a Jewish View of Natural Law," in *The Pursuit of the Ideal: Jewish Writings of Steven Schwarzschild*, ed. Menachem Kellner (Albany: SUNY Press, 1990), pp. 29-59, esp. p. 47.

42.　See below, p. 59.

43.　See Cohen's extensive discussion of the issue of the Noachite, pp. 37-43. The philosophical and textual issues involved are insightfully laid out by Schwarzschild, "Do Noachites Have to Believe in Revelation?"

44.　See below, p. 49.

45.　For Cohen's letter of "recommendation" for the unsuccessful candidate, see Robert S. Schine, *Jewish Thought Adrift: Max Wiener, 1882-1950* (Atlanta: Scholars Press, 1992), pp. 181-183.

46.　See below, p. 52.

47.　"The *Jewish faith*, as originally established, was only a collection of merely statutory laws supporting a political state; for whatever moral additions were *appended* to it, whether originally or only later, do not in any way belong to Judaism as such. Strictly speaking, Judaism is not a religion at all but simply the union of a number of individuals who, since they belonged to a particular stock, established themselves into a community under purely political laws, hence not into a church." Kant, *Religion Within the Boundaries of Mere Reason*, p. 130.

48.　Cohen, *Werke*, p. 414; *JS*, vol. 3, p. 363; below, p. 51.

49.　Following Rosenzweig's thesis that Cohen's late thought was animated by a "return" to Judaism, Ernst Simon seeks to connect this shift to Cohen's more polemical position on Spinoza. See Ernst Simon, "Zu Hermann Cohens Spinoza-Auffassung," in *Monatsschrift für die Geschichte und Wissenschaft des Judentums* (1935), pp. 181-194, reprinted in *Brücken: Gesammelte Aufsätze* (Heidelberg: Lambert Schneider, 1965), pp. 205-214, esp. p. 206. In finding the argument unpersuasive, I concur with Helmut

Holzhey, "Pantheismus, Ethik und Politik: Hermann Cohens Spinozakritik," in *6. Internationales Kongress der Spinoza-Gesellschaft* (Zurich: Schulthess, 2001), pp. 239-254, esp. p. 242 n. 1.

50.   Rosenzweig, introduction to "Ein ungedruckter Vortrag," p. 43.

51.   Leo Strauss, "Cohen's Analysis of Spinoza's Bible Science" (1924), in Leo Strauss, *The Early Writings (1921-1932)*, ed. and trans. Michael Zank (Albany: SUNY Press, 2002), pp. 140-172.

52.   Ibid., p. 158, and, for Cohen's "apologetic interest," p. 159.

53.   Sharing the assumption made by Carl Gebhardt in his biographical introduction to the German translation of the *Theological-Political Treatise*.

54.   For an account of Strauss' encounter with Hermann Cohen, see Thomas Meyer, *Zwischen Philosophie und Gesetz: Jüdische Philosophie und Theologie von 1933 bis 1938* (Leiden: Brill, 2007), ch. 1, esp. pp. 25ff. Strauss' 1924 response to Cohen prompted Julius Guttmann to offer him a research position at the *Hochschule für die Wissenschaft des Judentums* in Berlin for his work on Spinoza, which culminated in his book *Spinoza's Critique of Religion* (1930). In the preface to the 1965 English-language edition Strauss reflects that he wrote the book as a young man in the throes of the theological-political predicament. See Leo Strauss, *Spinoza's Critique of Religion*, trans. E.M. Sinclair (1965; reprint, Chicago: University of Chicago Press, 1997), p. 15.

55.   *Theological-Political Treatise*, end of ch. 3, "On the Election of the Hebrews." See below, p. 30, and footnote 156 for the Latin. The phrase "discourage manliness" is a translation of *effoeminarent*, which more accurately means "render womanlike."

56.   Buber's open letter was titled "Begriffe und Wirklichkeit" (Concepts and Reality). Cohen's response was "Antwort an das offene Schreiben des Herrn Dr. Martin Buber an Hermann Cohen," in *JS*, vol. 2, pp. 328-240, esp. p. 328. The main texts of the debate between Cohen and Buber are translated in "Martin Buber and Hermann Cohen: A Debate on Zionism and Messianism," in *The Jew in the Modern World: A Documentary History*, ed. Paul Mendes-Flohr and Jehudah Reinharz, 2nd ed. (New York: Oxford University Press, 1995), pp. 571-577. See the detailed account of the Cohen-Buber controversy in Wiedebach, *Die Bedeutung der Nationalität*, pp. 23-37.

57.   *JS*, vol. 2, p. 329.

58.   Rosenzweig, "Einleitung," in *JS*, vol. 1, p. lx: "Die Kerls wollen glücklich sein!"

59.   Ulrich Sieg, introduction to "Das Testament von Hermann und Martha Cohen," *Zeitschrift für Neuere Theologiegeschichte* 4 (1997), p. 260 and n. 37.

NOTES ON THE TRANSLATION

"SPINOZA ON STATE AND RELIGION, JUDAISM AND CHRISTIANITY"
("Spinoza über Staat und Religion, Judentum und Christentum") was first
published in 1915 in the *Jahrbuch für jüdische Geschichte und Literatur* by the
Verband der Vereine für jüdische Geschichte und Literatur in Deutschland
(Berlin: Poppelauer), 18:56-150, and was reprinted in 1924 in Cohen's *Jüdische
Schriften* (Berlin: C.A. Schwetschke), vol. 3, p. 290-372. This translation is based
on the critical edition of the German original in Hermann Cohen, *Werke*, vol.
16, *Kleinere Schriften V, 1913-1915*, ed. and introduced by Hartwig Wiedebach
(Hildesheim: Georg Olms Verlag, 1997), pp. 321-426.

Cohen made liberal use of italics to emphasize certain words and occasionally
entire sentences. His italics are preserved in this translation. He also italicized
words and phrases in his citations from Spinoza's Latin original; these have not
been preserved. In the Latin original of the *Theological-Political Treatise*, Spinoza
includes extensive citations from the Bible in the original Hebrew, before giving
the Latin translation. In the now-standard English translation of the *Theological-
Political Treatise*, by Samuel Shirley, the Hebrew citations have been omitted.

In his monograph on Spinoza, Cohen quotes at length from Carl Gebhardt's
German translation of the *Theological-Political Treatise*: Spinoza, *Theologisch-
politischer Traktat*, vol. 93 of *Philosophische Bibliothek*, 3rd ed. (Leipzig: Felix
Meiner, 1908). In the footnotes, Cohen usually provides the corresponding
passage in the original Latin, using the 1895 edition of J. van Vloten and J.P.N.
Land: Spinoza, *Opera*, 3 vols. For the English reader, I have substituted the
English translation from *Spinoza: Complete Works*, trans. Samuel Shirley, ed.
Michael L. Morgan (Indianapolis: Hackett, 2002). For the Latin citations I have
used the more recent and more accessible critical Latin edition by Carl Gebhardt,
Spinoza Opera, im Auftrag der Heidelberger Akademie der Wissenschaften (1925;
reprint, Heidelberg: Carl Winter, 1972). Where Cohen cites two passages that
occur in close proximity, I have occasionally collapsed two citations into one,
separated by an ellipsis. In some instances I have modified Shirley's translation
of the Latin to make it conform more closely to the German translation used by
Cohen; such changes are indicated in the footnotes. Any unbracketed ellipsis in
a Latin text was placed there by Cohen. A bracketed ellipsis indicates that Cohen

omitted part of the original in his citation. The shorthand [i.o.] ("in the original") indicates that Cohen's quotation differs from the original text he is citing.

Square brackets in the text indicate words or phrases that I have added for the sake of clarity. In Latin citations in the footnotes, square brackets indicate passages in the Latin that Cohen quoted in German translation but omitted from the footnotes in which he reproduced the corresponding Latin original.

Citations from the Jewish Bible are taken from *Tanakh: A New Translation of the Holy Scriptures According to the Traditional Hebrew Text* (Philadelphia and Jerusalem: The Jewish Publication Society, 1985).

KEY TO ABBREVIATIONS

Key to Endnotes

Unattributed footnotes are the original notes by Hermann Cohen.

CW   Spinoza, *Complete Works* with translations by Samuel Shirley. Edited with introduction and notes by Michael L. Morgan. Indianapolis/Cambridge: Hackett Publishing Co., 2002.

HW   Notes by Hartwig Wiedebach, editor of vol. 16 of the German critical edition of Hermann Cohen, *Werke*. Translated here by permission.

RSS   Notes added by the translator.

In this English edition, all three sets of notes are combined and numbered sequentially.

Pagination

|149| Numbers on the margins indicate the pagination in *Jüdische Schriften*, which are also found at the foot of the page in the modern critical edition of Cohen's *Werke*.

ACKNOWLEDGEMENTS

I AM GRATEFUL TO THE MANY FRIENDS and colleagues who offered help and advice in the course of my work on this translation: Rivi Handler-Spitz, Michael Katz, Jonathan Price, the late A. Joshua Sherman, and Jonathan Sisson. I owe special thanks to Peter Cole and Adina Hoffman for their critical review of the introduction; to Thomas Meyer for sharing his expertise on the history of German-Jewish thought from Cohen to its end and exile; to my research assistant, Shahar Fineberg, for correlating all of Cohen's Latin citations to Gebhardt's critical edition of Spinoza's works; and to Hartwig Wiedebach, the editor of the relevant volume of the German critical edition of Cohen's works. Wiedebach is responsible for the invaluable annotations adorning that German edition. He readily consented to their inclusion in the English translation, as did the general editor of the critical edition, Helmut Holzhey (Zurich). Wiedebach gave the introduction a critical reading and, along with my colleague Michael Geisler of Middlebury College, helped illuminate a few unusually obscure passages in Cohen's prose. I am grateful to the patient librarians who preside over the Judaica Reading Room of the National Library of Israel on the Givat Ram campus of the Hebrew University. I would also like to thank the fellows of the Shalem Center for a fruitful discussion of my introduction in their monthly seminar. Finally, I thank the copy editors, Judy Lee and Marian Rogers, the former editor of Shalem Press, Yael Hazony, and the manager of the Press, Marina Pilipodi.

Robert S. Schine
2013
Jerusalem / Middlebury

SPINOZA ON STATE AND RELIGION, JUDAISM AND CHRISTIANITY

SPINOZA OFFERS AN EXTENSIVE assessment of both the Old and New Testaments in the book that also contains his investigations on the concept of religion in relation to the concept of the state. The title of the book conjoins these two problems: *Theological-Political Treatise*. What is lacking, however, is any reference to philosophy, which after all may have a function, both in theology and in politics.

Before examining the logical coherence and appropriateness of this title more closely, we need to familiarize ourselves with the significance of Spinoza's book in its cultural and historical context. Its significance is twofold: the book served the universal promotion of the Enlightenment in both religion and politics. The book's literary value, then, exceeds perhaps even its systematic philosophical value. For as a *political treatise* it investigates the relationship between *church* and *state* from the perspective of the relationship between *religion* and *state*. And it is generally acknowledged that as a theological treatise, it is significant for having introduced *Bible criticism* into the discipline of theology.

As a first step, since recent discoveries[1] have convincingly altered the conventional wisdom that Spinoza led a solitary life, we have to see the *Treatise* in its biographical and historical context. The *Theological-Political Treatise* is a manifesto advocating the republican politics of Johan de Witt.[2]

|291|
"The true reason for the composition of the *Theological-Political Treatise* is Spinoza's relationship to Johan de Witt." The author of this statement makes the same claim concerning the *Tractatus Politicus*, "that this work, in its practical aspect, is nothing other than a Dutch political tract in support of the politics of Johan de Witt. Similarly, the *Theological-Political Treatise* offers a defense of the policies of the councilor pensionary[3] toward the church."[4] The same author thus gives credence to the report, originating with Spinoza's biographer, Lucas,[5] that Spinoza received a pension in the amount of 200 florins from Johan de Witt, and he concludes that, "given the extraordinary sensitivity" for which Spinoza was known, "he must have had a very close relationship to the man whom he allowed to relieve him of the cares of life."[6] This close relationship, however, bears on a very complex and essential issue, in which religion and state collide.

How, then, in terms of topical arrangement, are we to make sense of the fact that Spinoza has combined a publicistic purpose with a purely philological question[7]—that of the date of composition, the authorship, and the redactors of the individual books of the Bible—and construed the two tasks as the topic of one and the same book? The two really appear to have no imaginable connection. And if they are nonetheless treated together in one book, one would have to be led *a priori* to the suspicion that, since the combination itself is unnatural, the investigation was not carried out with the requisite neutrality, either with regard to both of these tasks or at least with regard to one of them. For either the political inquiry has suffered, anticipating the theological issue, or the latter has suffered as a result of its linkage to the political theory that Spinoza attempts to formulate. At the very least, one of the two tasks has forfeited something of its *independent* objectivity.

In fact, Bible criticism would not have entered into this book if the path had not been prepared by another moment in Spinoza's life. It is well known that Spinoza was placed under a writ of [major] excommunication by the synagogue in Amsterdam. We believe we may refrain from taking any position at all here on the question of principle regarding the legitimacy of excommunication. Moreover, the specific reason that the synagogue imposed |292| this penalty will emerge later of its own accord and does not concern the precautions the Jewish community might have taken to protect itself against potential informers, a distinct type in the history of Jewish persecution. Our present concern is solely to assess the connection between this biographical fact and the composition of the *Theological-Political Treatise*.

Spinoza composed a protest titled "Apologia" against the ban under which he had been placed, and the work was circulated and read by friends.[8] Apparently he refrained from publishing the piece because it was his intention to take on his opponents in a work of greater scope and broader perspective. Perhaps he may also have derived a kind of dual satisfaction from the thought that he would wage his battle against both Judaism and its biblical sources at one and the same time, in keeping with the spirit of his politics. In that case, however, he must have had no doubt that there was a vital connection between his politics, both in its goals and in its conceptual assumptions, and his actual philosophy, his *Ethics*. Otherwise, the omission of philosophy in the title of the work would be an ominous sign. For the *Treatise* itself leaves no doubt that the basic ideas of the *Ethics* were well established at the time of the former's composition. This raises the interesting question of whether the basic ideas of the *Treatise* are consistent not just with the political orientation of the times, but also with the *Ethics*, the work that contains Spinoza's entire philosophy.

And now a clear and decisive reason for refraining from publishing the "Apologia" does emerge—a reason that is also apparent in the organization of the *Treatise*. The *Treatise* consists of twenty chapters. Not until *chapter 16* do we find the title "The Basis of the State." Following that, *chapter 17* treats "The Hebrew State." And *chapter 18* continues, "From the commonwealth of the Hebrews and their history..." The two final chapters are the first to deal purely theoretically with law in religious matters and with freedom of conscience.

From a universal cultural standpoint the two final chapters constitute the historical and political value of the Treatise. On their account the *Treatise* is one of the *foundational works of political-religious liberalism.*　|293| We will not go into the question of whether, from this standpoint, Spinoza may have had predecessors, not wishing to belittle his own achievement. We mention here only that Hobbes, when asked for his judgment on the *Treatise*, very tellingly responded: "Judge not, that ye be not judged."[9] So complete was his identification with his successor.[10] We, however, will have to determine whether this liberalism, first in the form in which it appears in Spinoza's *Ethics* and then in the spirit of his ethical theory of the state and ethical theory of religion, resolves or even advances *the ethical problem*. But for the time being, we are still in the midst of a review of the table of contents of the *Treatise* and must leave aside these fundamental questions.

From *chapter 12* on, Spinoza treats the general questions of *natural theology*. Up to that point, however, nearly two-thirds of the entire book is concerned with *biblical theology*. And *chapter 13*, on the quintessence of biblical teaching, should actually be included as well. We will see, however, that the entire theological content of Spinoza's Bible criticism is directed at the state of the Hebrews, that is, at the idea that the *religion* of Judaism founded by Moses set for itself the sole purpose of establishing and preserving the Jewish *state*. *That is the basis and core of this entire philological inquiry*.[11] It is aimed at the destruction of the Jewish concept of religion and is thus guided and motivated by a *philosophical* assumption. Therefore, whereas the basic motive of Spinoza's critique of the Jewish religion was philosophical, there was still an entirely historical, publicistic reason for this philosophical critique.

|294| Spinoza wants to demonstrate that the state of the Hebrews is the source of all orthodox evil, and thus a threat to freedom of thought. In keeping with the spirit of the liberal regents' party, he seeks to defend the policies of de Witt against the preachers of the orthodox party of the supporters of the House of Orange. The *Treatise* was printed at the very press "that also produced literature in support of de Witt."[12] One polemic written against the *Treatise* stated that it had been "hatched in Hell by the apostate Jew in concert with the devil, and published with the knowledge of Mister Jan and his accomplices." Concerning this "discussion of Judaism," which, after all, constitutes the main part of the book, the author whom we quote repeatedly here states "that these deliberations are only loosely connected to his actual purpose, and that in the book we have before us Spinoza's *original defense* against... the accusations against him, even if in revised form." He is content to take Spinoza's polemical stance as sufficient explanation for the "severe, even hostile judgments" that Spinoza passes "on the nation from which he himself hails... In battle, justice is no virtue." But what of his judgment, not about the nation, but about the *religion* of this nation? A man may pass a "severe, even hostile judgment" on a nation; but a philosopher ought to take responsibility for his judgment on religion.

Our author does not pose this question. And I might also say: *No one else* has taken a position on this question. Yet it concerns not just the Jewish religion, and not just religion in general: there is a further problem both for Spinoza as publicist and certainly for Spinoza as philosopher. We have already considered the complications in which Spinoza's literary project is entangled. Ultimately it is apparent that he harbored a grievance about his excommunication, which he pours forth in his treatise on political philosophy, using a philological investigation into the Bible as the basis of his tract. And now it is also apparent that the entire critique of the Bible was, in the end, a critique of the Jewish state. Furthermore, however deeply grounded the systematic basis of the *Treatise*, its actual historical motive was the opportunity that presented itself to publish a political manifesto.

In such a tangle of prejudices, there are serious risks to the objectivity and impartiality of even the greatest writer, to say nothing of a writer intent on working off an old grievance. We have already cited one impartial source |295| for the view that Spinoza's judgments are "severe, even hostile." How could someone who is "hostile" toward his own nation undertake to disclose and describe the character of Judaism from biblical sources? Such a person may be able to shed light on the date and sequence of the books of the Bible. Those accomplishments are clear enough. But Bible criticism would be in a sorry state if it consisted only of philological analysis of this kind; if, for its *understanding* of the Bible, and in particular for its understanding of the *Prophets*, it were actually based, intellectually, on Spinoza. C. Siegfried's conclusive findings have freed biblical scholarship from the dangers of this kind of prejudice.[13]

Our question must go further still. If Spinoza's judgment both as politician and as biblical scholar was biased, then what may we expect of him as philosopher, as ethicist, in defining the relationship between state and religion? That relationship is inseparable, in turn, from the relationship between religion and *philosophy*, and therefore also from the relationship between state and philosophy.

What does Spinoza give as a definition of religion? This is the first consequence of this unnatural configuration of questions: in defining the concept of religion Spinoza does not take his *Ethics* as his point of departure; rather, he derives the concept from *Scripture*, unambiguously equating the concept of religion with the content of Scripture, which consists of the so-called word of God. Thus Spinoza construes several concepts as *identical*: |296| *the word of God, revelation, universal religion, divine law,* and *faith.*

Faith is a kind of knowledge, a subjective relationship of the human mind to the truth, in particular to the knowledge of God as the primary basis of truth. In monotheism, therefore, religion means simply *faith in God.* And since faith is a kind of knowledge, faith in God must have, as its content, the concept of God. It is less important whether this concept encompasses the essence or substance of God, or is limited to his *attributes*. The *concept* of God still constitutes the content, the object of faith.

All *knowledge* is conditioned by its object. But faith, more than all other knowledge, would be empty and void of all content if the concept of God were removed from it, if it were not recognized as having, in relation to the concept of God, the general character of knowledge.

Spinoza has the distinction of having produced such a useless concept of religion that it altogether excludes the knowledge of God from faith. According to Spinoza, Scripture teaches only "that God exists, one alone and omnipotent God... But what God is... and similar matters, Scripture does not teach formally, and as eternal doctrine."[14] Scripture "never expressly gives a *definition* of God... All this leads us to the conclusion that the intellectual knowledge of God... has no bearing on... faith and on revealed religion, and |297| that consequently man can go far astray."[15] What emerges here is a *tension between faith and knowledge*.

However, since knowledge relates here not to the objects of *science*, as it would have to according to Descartes—that is, it would be connected, in a precise way, to mathematics—this tension extends to reason in general. Spinoza severs faith, and thus Scripture too, entirely from reason. As a consequence, there can also be no error for faith.

This was Spinoza's plan from the beginning. For we know that it was his aim to liberate philosophy from the church. He seeks to accomplish this liberation by denying any relationship whatsoever between reason and Scripture as the charter of the church, because Scripture does not and should not have anything "in common with philosophy."[16] Now what sort of a faith and what sort of a religion can that be if it denies any connection to knowledge of God, and thus to reason altogether? And at this point we may pose a further question: What concept of the *state* can possibly result if the state, in order to assert its sovereignty over the church, must empty the latter of its divine lifeblood and sap it of all knowledge?

It is characteristic of minds like Spinoza's that they construct their ideas for the sake of public effect, to have an effect on a current issue. They do not shrink from conclusions that might prompt them to reexamine their premises. On the contrary, the very paradox of such conclusions fascinates them, because it offers them the illusion that they are showing courage in battle. We have to ask first: What can the *content* of *faith* be if knowledge of God is excluded?

For Spinoza, faith is *obedience* to God. Thus faith produces or signifies not a theoretical relationship to God, but only a practical one. Yet how is human *action* possible if it is not guided by reason, which, for Spinoza in any event, is synonymous with will? Spinoza's defense against this objection—but what a defense for a *philosophical* grounding of religion—is to equate *faith with revelation*, with Scripture. The will, purportedly, cannot |298| be motivated by reason, whereas it can be motivated by Scripture! Thus an ambiguity emerges: that Scripture, which is supposed to have nothing in common with philosophy, is nevertheless equated, with regard to the will, with reason. "However, I found in that which Scripture *explicitly* teaches nothing that would not conform to reason or that would contradict it."[17] *Reason thus has a double meaning: it is both the faculty of knowledge*[18] *and a faculty that is part of the will.* Aside from that, however, Spinoza stands by his negation and thus sees no need at all to confront the question of the relationship, in positive terms, between Scripture and reason.[19]

However, if there were such a positive relationship [between Scripture and reason], even if only in a limited and qualified way, would not knowledge, by way of reason, then reenter the realm of faith after all? And would not faith then no longer be limited to *obedience*? After all, from a psychological perspective, obedience hovers between heaven and earth: it cannot begin to act unless spurred and guided by knowledge. Spinoza calls the doctrine of obedience "the aim of Scripture." "Who can fail to see that both the Testaments are simply a training for obedience? [...] Moses' aim was to convince the Israelites not by reasoned argument, but rather... [by using] means to promote obedience, not to impart knowledge. The message of the Gospel is one of simple faith... obedience to God."[20]

Here we must stop to ask: If the concept of religion is a question of the distinction between obedience on the one hand and knowledge or reason on the other, then what, in the context of this distinction, is the meaning of the *sciences*?[21] True, Moses did not set about to teach obedience by means of the sciences, but it does not follow that he had no intent whatsoever to base |299| obedience on knowledge or reason. With the sciences' sudden appearance on the scene, one recognizes that the entire problem is, by its very nature, connected to philosophy: it is for the sake of philosophy that religion must be separated from reason, because philosophy must be separated from the church. Philosophy is supposed to find protection *only in the state*. Because of this goal, religion has to be adapted to the state and thus limited to the practical realm. To be sure, for the Spinoza of the *Ethics* this is an utter contradiction; for him there is no discrete realm of praxis, because there is no discrete will: "*intellectus et voluntas unum et idem sunt*."[22]

As early as the preface of the *Treatise*, Spinoza equates this otherwise practical consequence with the "simple concepts of the divine mind[23] as it was revealed to the prophets; that is—to obey God with all one's heart by practicing justice and charity."[24] Yet even here Spinoza is already drawing a distinction between revealed and "natural" knowledge, with respect both to its object and to "its basis and its method."[25] This is the rigid and sharp separation he makes between revelation and knowledge, where the basis and method of the latter lie in *reason*. Thus he comes to the conclusion that "faith alone without works is dead."[26] And, following John, he defines *the spirit of God* as love, which, in turn, he equates with *obedience*. From this position he draws a conclusion that not only disagrees with Paul: more than that, he *places religion completely outside the realm of truth*.

This conclusion is the result of his useful separation of religion and reason: "Finally, it follows that faith requires not so much *true* dogmas as *pious* dogmas, that is, such as move the heart to obedience; and this is so even if many of those beliefs contain not a *shadow of a truth*, provided that he who adheres to them knows not that they are false... Hence it follows |300| *that* a catholic or universal faith must *not contain any dogmas* that good men may regard as *controversial*."[27] Where, however, is the *criterion* for such a harmony of opinion among good men? Spinoza says not that there may be no dogmas in a universal faith, but only none that qualify according to a criterion he has not set forth.

Moreover, he has no qualms about the consequences of his pragmatism: "for such dogmas may be to one man pious, to another impious, since their value lies only in the works they inspire."[28] This, then, is the deeper meaning of the sentence "Dogmas should only be practical rules of obedience."[29] What is lacking, unfortunately, is an explanation of the intellectual cord that connects such works inspired by dogma.

Of course, this theory is bound to dissolve into a series of absurd contradictions. Spinoza lists his dogmas, of which the first is "God... exists... He who knows not, or does not believe, that God exists cannot obey him."[30] Thus, just as existence presupposes something of the essence, obedience presupposes knowledge, which, however, is plainly left undefined. "He who knows not, or does not believe." Knowledge is simply supposed to vanish from view, behind faith. Yet faith is still an indispensable kind of knowledge.

The dogma of the existence of God is not the end of the matter. The second dogma is "God is *one alone*."[31] But is it not the case that the

uniqueness of God is based on cognition?[32] Our expert in Jewish philosophy | 301 |
of religion makes no mention of the fact that uniqueness is a problem of
cognition alone. There is no mention that the distinction between cognition
and perception is, in relation to uniqueness, just as sharp and clear as it
has been since Parmenides and Plato. Spinoza surrenders the dogma of
the uniqueness of God to faith as universal religion, yet he separates this
religion from cognition and reason.

At this point a gap opens up in the continuity of religious philosophical
reflection. It may provide a sad but adequate explanation for the substantive
chaos in Spinoza's views.

First, let us follow the conclusions Spinoza has drawn: "But as to the
question of what God, the exemplar of true life, really is, whether he is
fire, spirit, light, thought, or something else, this is irrelevant to faith. And
so likewise is the question as to why he is the exemplar of true life... In
these questions it matters not what beliefs a man holds."[33] Is it really all one
and the same, in what way and by what conceptual rationale God can be
[understood as] "the exemplar of true life"? Could God really be such an
exemplar in the same way as fire, spirit, or thought? This kind of philosophy
of religion is, in itself, entirely incomprehensible. It can be explained, as we
will see, only on the basis of the connection between this question of dogma
and Spinoza's *biblical exegesis*.

Yet even here he uses this idea to argue the contrary view as well:
"For we have shown that faith demands piety rather than truth."[34] Then he
observes: "How salutary this doctrine is, and how necessary in the state..."[35]
For the state, however, only philosophy should serve as knowledge.
"Philosophy rests on the basis of *universally valid axioms*... whereas faith |302|
is based on history and language and must be derived only from Scripture
and revelation."[36] Thus concludes the discussion of this distinction. Spinoza
does away as well with the universal axioms, the rational foundations, that
the Arabic and Jewish philosophers had established as the basis of faith.
Faith is obedience. Practice is not theory. The theory of practice, however,
is philosophy alone.

This position would be understandable if Spinoza were consistent and
were also to argue that religion cannot lead to practice, because cognition
alone must always be the guide. But then the Bible could not achieve its
identity with faith, and the goal here is that the Bible be authenticated, by its
"actual" content, as the "word of God." We know that this is the main topic
of the *Tractatus*. For this reason Spinoza cannot allow the conclusion that

religion is excluded: he has to make do with his critique of rational biblical interpretation, or at most argue against Maimonides, and likewise against R. Judah Alpachar. "We may therefore conclude without reservation that neither must Scripture be made to conform with reason, nor reason with Scripture... I maintain absolutely that this fundamental dogma of theology cannot be investigated by the natural light of reason."[37] What remains, when the natural light has been extinguished, Spinoza then calls "moral certainty." Yet how can any kind of certainty be admissible that does not proceed from natural light?[38]

This is the kind of religion, deprived of natural reason, that Spinoza establishes here as *natural* and *universal* religion. Moreover, the welfare of the state is purported to rest on it. What view of the state results from this derivation of faith? What kind of freedom within the state follows from obedience to God? And can philosophy somehow supersede, for the state, this irrational obedience? Moreover, can philosophy do this when |303| an irreconcilable opposition between religion and philosophy destroys the unity of culture? *Such a conception of religion throws into question the very concept of the state.*

Since the Renaissance, the theory of the state has been based on the concept of *nature*. As early as the age of the glory of Greece, *nature* meant *original truth*. Plato defended law and justice against the Sophists. He defended knowledge and its certainty, as based on nature, against the Skeptics, who equated state and law with power, convention, and custom. Thus, from the beginning, law and state have opposed nature and power.

The eternal value of nature was demonstrated and reaffirmed by the Stoics. The Renaissance, in turn, revived the cultural-historical approach of the Stoics and applied it to all the questions of reform in the modern era. This is the reason for the appearance of *natural religion* alongside *natural law*. Nature was considered to be both the historical basis and the intellectual root of all historical cultural institutions. A distinction was made between historical changes on the one hand and nature as their abiding basis on the other.

However, even in this fundamental Stoic concept of nature there is a certain ambiguity, which arises from the part the Stoics played in the development of *pantheism*. And in Spinoza this ambiguity becomes a major annoyance. In Spinoza, after all, nature equals God (*deus sive natura*). Hence nature belongs to the same category as *substance*. It represents that which is *original* and *abiding* in everything natural, as well as in everything intellectual and ethical. At this point we will not consider the difficulties this position presents for the problem of *knowledge*; they should just be noted. Yet the supposed absence of any distinction between God and nature compromises the concept of the spirit of *ethics* even more than it compromises the concept of the spirit of knowledge. Religion, law, and state may then be conceived of as nature in the Stoic sense—that is, as that which is original and eternal in that problematic historical fact.[39] |304|

In this context, however, the secondary concept[40] of nature may be interjected into theory and practice and may occasionally be promoted to the primary concept in relation to these questions. When this occurs, it does so insofar as this concept of nature derives the historical development of law and the state from the nature of the human economy and from the nature of commerce between nations. In that case, the old, contrary Sophistic concept of *power as nature* has reappeared, and the fundamental ethical power of nature yields to the power [of nature] based on natural law, the power present in climate, as in the entire natural history of men and nations.[41]

Moreover, the validity that nature had acquired through the concept of natural law in modern times gave Spinoza additional grounds for his equation of nature and God. Nature represented not only the *substance of being*, but also *the necessity of law*. Thus all truth could be encompassed in the concept of nature. The laws of nature are the *eternal truths* and necessities of being, *all* being; for *all being is God*. No species of being may be separated or set apart from God. Anything ethical, therefore, as well as anything natural, is grounded in and made necessary by the eternal laws of nature. Thus law and state must also be contained in the laws of nature and in the *power* of its being.

The Sophistic character of this concept of nature is plainly evident in Spinoza when he sets about in *chapter 16* to establish the basis of the state on "the natural right of the individual" "before giving any consideration to the state and to religion."[42] Whereas Plato states that it is possible to derive the concept of man only from the concept of the state, it is characteristic of all Sophism to begin with this fictitious concept of the individual, because the individual is presented in *perception*, not thought, and *in an isolated experience*, not historical theory. Indeed, God exists in all his individual *modi*. The more we know individual things, the more we know |305|
God. Pantheism is based on *induction* and, therefore, is also based on inductionist illusions.

"By the right and established order of Nature I mean simply the rules governing the nature of every individual thing."[43] But are these rules identical for every individual? "For example, fish are determined by nature to swim, and the big ones to eat the smaller ones. Thus it is by sovereign natural right that fish inhabit water, and the big ones eat the smaller ones. For it is certain... that *Nature's right is coextensive with its power*. For Nature's power is the very power of God, who has sovereign right over all things."[44] From the start the entire arsenal of the *Ethics* is assembled here: nature and the individual, law and power, and above all, God.

It is understood: neither nature nor therefore God has any significance in itself that goes beyond a mere conceptual definition. Each is nothing more than the *aggregate concept* of all individuals. All being and all power proceed from individuals, and thus all law as well. "But since the universal power of Nature as a whole is nothing but the power of all individual things taken together, it follows that *each individual thing has the sovereign right to do all that it can do*; i.e., the right of the individual is coextensive with its determinate power."[45] *Right is therefore nature understood as the power of the individual.* Thus nature and the individual are identical.

|306| There is also no distinction among individuals in nature: "And here I do not acknowledge any distinction between men and other individuals of nature."[46] For this state of nature Spinoza cites *Paul*, "who declares that prior to the law... there can be no sin."[47] This is *the law of the state of nature* and its innocence.

Yet it is precisely this state of nature that is supposed to be overcome. At the same time, the question is whether, in this abstraction [i.e., in this concept of the state of nature —RSS], *reason* was ignored. That seems, in fact, to be the intent: "For not all men are naturally determined to act in accordance with the rules and laws of reason."[48] At this point, a sharp contradiction arises between *nature* and its possible laws on the one hand and the laws of *reason* on the other. How can nature, how can God, account for this difference among human beings?

Spinoza concludes from this [concept of the] law of nature[49] that it "does not frown on strife, or hatred, or anger, [or deceit,] or on anything at all urged by appetite."[50] "The bounds" of the eternal laws of nature "are not set by the laws of human reason..."[51] Here, once again, is the sharp contrast between nature and reason. "So when something in Nature appears to us as ridiculous, absurd, or *evil*..."[52] We will stop here. Do the ridiculous and the evil really evoke equal degrees of consternation? The distinction made here between nature as a whole and *our* nature is untenable. For all the astronomy in the world cannot prevent us, within our own microcosm, from labeling evil as such. Again, the ambiguity lies within "our" nature: whether what is meant is our nature that we have in common with *fish*, or |307| our nature as distinguished by the human capacity for the ethical.

Now that the condition of man in the state of nature has been established in that characteristically Sophistic way, the *state* is supposed to evolve from it. Utility, fear, passions, and desires bring the state into being. One of the "eternal truths" is the principle of choice between the lesser of two evils. And since the individual is in conflict with other individuals, I have to train my own power to accommodate the power of others. "We may thus conclude that the validity of a contract rests on its utility."[53] *The utility of a contract, then, is the basis of the right of the state.*

The state comprises the right of all individuals. By means of the mutual contract into which everyone has entered, every individual has transferred his natural right to the state. *The state, therefore, is subject to the same ambiguity as attaches, for Spinoza, to being, all substance, and all of nature.* The state is not a unity, sovereign over the whole, but only the sum of all individuals. Here Spinoza's concept of democracy emerges: "It is therefore defined as a universal union of human beings that corporately possesses sovereign right over everything within its power."[54] Once again, it is evident that this form of government is based on power. But how can the universality of this union be justified if it is sovereign only "*collegialiter*" ["corporately"]? The individuals and their state of nature have been transferred into the alleged universality of political democracy. Here, however, democracy is still the preferred political form: "I have elected to discuss [democracy] before all others because it seemed the most natural form of state, approaching most closely to that freedom which nature grants to every man."[55] At this point, Spinoza still advocates democracy.

By contrast, in the Tractatus Politicus *democracy must yield to aristocracy.* |308| The reason for this change in Spinoza's political persuasion is important for understanding his fundamental religious outlook. "...We have seen that the path taught by reason is a very difficult one, so that those who believe that ordinary people or those who are busily engaged in public business can be persuaded to live solely at reason's behest are dreaming of the poets' golden age or of a fairy tale."[56] But then would *ethics*, too, be banished to the land of fairy tales? Or does ethics insist on the distinction between the philosophers and the reason of the masses?

Because of this difference, democracy of course could not be sustained, and aristocracy had to take its place. "The latter must, by necessity, be eternal."[57] And now, by contrast, democracy becomes the "absolute state."[58] We will not pursue these questions further, to say nothing of their connection with Spinoza's advocacy for *de Witt*. We will focus only on the one idea: *that the masses are set up in opposition to the prescriptions of reason.*

This idea, which *rules out, on principle, the application of ethics to politics*, is hinted at in the concluding statements of the *Theological-Political Treatise*. We will also recognize that it is a basic motif in the historical section of the *Treatise*. Initially it may appear that the *Treatise*, a brief for the regents' party, only takes up the cause of religious enlightenment, freedom of religious discussion, and philosophy. Yet it was suspect from the start that Johan de Witt had *forbidden any connection between theology and philosophy*. An anonymous tract taking the contrary position had been published, and that work "caused a great sensation. The author of the book was his friend |309| *Ludwig Meyer*... With his *Theological-Political Treatise*, Spinoza intervened in this controversy, siding with Johan de Witt against Ludwig Meyer." This is reported in the introduction cited frequently above.[59]

If philosophy is separated from theology by its own *decree*, then there is no provision for religious *liberalism*. Moreover, a barrier is erected between public education and scientific thought, of which philosophy is a part. Instead, philosophy is relegated to a learned guild. This distinction between universal education and scientific inquiry is thus a fundamental defect of this theory of the state, and likewise of this theory of religion. The *state* must remain an *aristocracy*, because the masses are incapable of living according to reason. And religion must teach only obedience; it is to have absolutely nothing in common with speculative ideas. Both *religion and the state are void of reason, both for the same reason*. Spinoza draws this explicit conclusion concerning the relationship of the state to religion.

Up to this point, only faith or religion and the state have been under discussion, but no mention has been made of the church. The church, however, is the target of the entire manifesto and all its theories. It is on account of the church that not only religion, but also the scientific study of theology must be severed from all philosophy, because philosophy, like all the sciences, is cultivated by the state alone. Thus, state and church are, *a priori*, incompatible. What, then, is the relationship of the church to the state of nature?

This question leads us back to the other: What is the relationship of religion to the state of nature?

The state of nature knows no law. Thus, it cannot know any *divine* law either. And in God's book the only religion that is taught is revealed religion. In this book there is no natural religion. If, because of its simple content, a religion appears to be natural religion and even presents itself as such, it will always be equated with revelation. Spinoza says explicitly of the state of nature: "[it] is prior to religion in nature and in time."[60] "Therefore, |310| prior to revelation nobody can be bound by a divine law of which he cannot be aware... Therefore we must concede without qualification that the divine law began from the time when men by express covenant promised to obey God in all things, thereby... transferring their right to God in the manner we described in speaking of the civil state."[61] Just like the law of the *state*, so too divine law is based on *contract*, on the *transfer of natural freedom to God*.

What, then, is the relationship of the state to this divine power? The alternatives are the following: Either the state absorbs divine law into itself, or it exists parallel to it, as a law on its own. Or it subordinates itself to divine law as the superior power. The latter two possibilities create thorny complications for the state. "And if the sovereign power refuses to obey God as revealed in his Law, he may do so to his own peril and hurt without any violation of right, civil or natural."[62] Consequently the state does *not* recognize any civil right belonging to religion. That is the purpose of the entire *Treatise*: *to establish the right of the state to issue laws concerning religious belief, against the claims of the church.*

Thus it is manifest that the two contracts are irreconcilable: the contract with God concerning religion and the contract with the state concerning supreme power. This latter power is superior to divine right. Despite all the concessions that may be made to counter this claim, it is therefore superior to God. What, then, is meant by *the kingdom of God*? The definition of the kingdom of God is as follows: "that the kingdom of God is where justice and charity have the force of law and command... So if I now show that |311| justice and charity can acquire the force of law and command only through the right of the state, I can readily draw the conclusion... that religion can acquire the force of law only from the decree of those who have the right to command, and that God has no special kingdom over men save through the medium of those who hold the sovereignty."[63] *Thus the kingdom of God becomes the particular state.* And this idea is expressed repeatedly: "[all the precepts of true reason, including] charity toward one's neighbor, acquire the force of law and command only from the right of the state."[64] "We cannot doubt that, as soon as the Hebrews transferred their right to the king of Babylon, the kingdom of God and the divine law *came to an abrupt end*."[65]

In formulations of the most explicit kind, repeated again and again, Spinoza thus accomplishes the *distinction between state and church*, extending to the very ethical and religious foundations of the church. To be sure, it is another question whether the concepts are defined precisely enough to allow such a sharp distinction. How is the state supposed to foster justice and love if it also reserves the right, by virtue of its supreme power, to violate them, as divine law, "at its own risk and to its own detriment"?[66] It may be said that *this question* is left unresolved.

From these political-theoretical assumptions, Spinoza set about the *third task* that he sought to address in this single work. The *first* task was to produce a manifesto for de Witt. The *second* task, connected to the first, |312| was to defend freedom of thought and the religious enlightenment against ecclesiastical orthodoxy. If we disregard the peculiar, biographical bias in his apologia against Judaism, then only one purely *scientific* task remains: *Bible criticism*. However, the objectivity of his Bible criticism may be compromised as well, not only by the biographical factor and his intended rejoinder to Judaism, but no less by his *political theory*.

For someone who equates divine law with the civil state, *the religion of the prophets* must mean revolt and revolution. On occasion Spinoza remarks that these "men of private station", the prophets, "succeeded in annoying men rather than reforming them, whereas men who were admonished or castigated by kings were more apt to turn from their ways. Indeed, even devout kings often found prophets intolerable..."[67] Thus, the prophets have done "more harm than good," and "great civil wars also originated" on their account.[68] It is all logical: the prophets were "men of private station." As such, they could not teach religion, which only the state may decree. What, then, is the relationship of these men of private station to *revelation*? Does God have *other* messengers and intermediaries, aside from the prophets, to reveal his divine law?

This question is decisive for Spinoza's attitude toward *Christianity*, as distinct from and in contrast to his attitude toward Judaism. To be sure, the structure of the *Treatise* is such that this difference is not discussed in any particular chapters. Instead, because Spinoza maintains *the unity of the two Testaments,* the distinction comes to light *only in his characterization of the prophets as distinct from Christ.*

With "revelation or prophecy" we have arrived at the *first chapter* of this book, "Of Prophecy." The discussion opens with an equation: "Prophecy, *or* revelation."[69] The *second chapter* is titled "Of the Prophets." Nonetheless, in the chapter on prophecy, it is already stated: "A prophet is one who..."[70] For a |313| work that is supposed to represent the beginning of modern Bible criticism, the beginning is still rather primitive. For we would have expected that a discussion of the concept of prophecy would begin with the distinction between the *literary* documents and prophecy in the form of oracles. Yet here prophecy is defined as "*sure* knowledge of some matter revealed by God to man."[71] On the other hand, one now has to ask: Is prophecy, as "sure knowledge," science and philosophy, or is there sure knowledge aside from philosophy?

It follows from this definition of prophecy that "natural knowledge can be called prophecy."[72] At this point objections must be raised from all sides. First, we have already established that there is no God in the *state of nature*: how, then, could there be natural knowledge of prophecy? The meaning of *nature* in this context must therefore be different from its meaning in the state of nature. A further reservation must be registered: Spinoza appears to be mocking when he equates prophecy with natural knowledge, when prophecy, after all, is revelation and thus divine knowledge!

Rational understanding can neither illuminate nor overcome such difficulties. Only the history of philosophy can shed light in this darkness. It was Descartes who used several terms to indicate his "principle of certainty." One of them is *nature*, or, to use the scholastic expression, "*natural light*."[73] On the other hand, he also *equates this* concept of nature with the concept of God.[74] Both are principles of certainty, just like the "I" (*moi-même*) in the *Cogito*. All these terms are synonymous with the methodological term of the *general rule*.[75]

Thus, when Spinoza equates prophecy with natural knowledge, he does so because prophecy was defined as certain knowledge. It can acquire its certainty, however, only from the *criterion* of nature, from nature conceived of as a criterion. Consequently, here too knowledge of nature becomes knowledge of God. "[F]or the knowledge that we acquire by the natural |314| light of reason depends solely on knowledge of God and of his eternal decrees."[76] Thus revelation is *natural* knowledge on the basis of the criterion of nature, and, at the same time, it is *divine* knowledge on the basis of the criterion of God. In the one case the prophets possess knowledge; in the other case they are only interpreters. Spinoza employs the latter term to render the Hebrew nabi.[77]

With this equation of natural knowledge and prophecy, a new ambiguity once again arises in the concept of prophecy: Is prophecy knowledge or only a mouthpiece? Prophecy is to enjoy no superiority over natural knowledge, which likewise can be called divine knowledge. Here *pantheism* comes into play again: for natural knowledge "is dictated to us, as it were, by God's nature insofar as we participate therein, and by God's decrees."[78] This is not what *Descartes* meant by the equivalence of nature and God as a criterion of certainty. Nevertheless, this allusion is developed further. One can already see, however, that prophetic knowledge is to be recognized as divine only in the sense that it is *natural* for *all* human beings, insofar as all human beings participate in God's nature. But the other meaning of nature is the actual point here: prophetic knowledge is not superior in any way to the knowledge of the rest of humanity.

In this context Spinoza's *basic exegetical rule* should help: the Bible is to be explained *solely from itself*. And above all it should be noted that "the Jews never make mention of intermediate or particular causes, or pay any heed to them, but... they refer everything to God."[79] This is how we are to understand that the prophets are not somehow the literary authors of their thoughts, but that everything was revealed to the prophets, "either by words, or by appearance, or by a combination of both."[80] The literary point of view is not considered here at all; for how could a revelation, a communication, occur at all except by means of words in which the visions or appearances are immediately translated? This definition [of prophecy] cannot have been reached without some ulterior motive; it must point toward some distinction. But if prophecy is simply revelation, what revelation could then be distinguished from prophecy?

|315|

And if it is correct that prophetic *knowledge* should be limited by this definition, then could some divine revelation make use of any means other than words and visions? Would prophecy not then become moot, and, with it, the concept of *revelation*?

Here too only the style and character of the book can serve as a guide to understanding. We have already touched on the issue of the significance of the prophets for the state. What matters here is the state and its omnipotence; religion is secondary, since it must derive its legitimacy from the state. *The prophecy of the Old Testament is, therefore, along with the entire religion of the Old Testament*, reduced to a religion of words, inasmuch as religion is based on prophecy. Of what, however, does knowledge consist, if not of words?

The issue here is apparently the *distinction between perception and knowledge*. Words and forms are means of *perception*. And *imagination* itself, which Spinoza, following an old convention, also ascribes to the prophets, is a form of *representation*[81] that is based, in turn, on perception. Now, in the psychology of religion, that may well pass as a rationalist explanation, as long as the *source* of the imagination is not somehow located in God, as if imagination proceeded from God. *However, it is such a corporeal personification of God that is the very meaning of this conception of prophecy.*

The prophets heard a real *voice*, and Moses was no exception. "With a real voice God revealed to Moses the laws..."[82] From Exodus 25:22, which he cites in Hebrew,[83] Spinoza claims to prove that "God employed a real voice."[84] Likewise in I Samuel 3. He also discusses the revelation at *Sinai*. "Some Jews take the view that the words of the Decalogue were not pronounced by God..."[85] Since the Decalogue is repeated in Deuteronomy, he himself assumes as much, that only a sound, not words, was heard there. Nevertheless, the matter stands: "...what the Israelites heard was a real voice; for in Deuteronomy 5:4 it expressly says, 'The Lord talked with you face to face.'"[86] Now one can see why he claims that the prophets heard the real voice of God: God really has a face. Spinoza's kind of literal philology does not consider it possible that the Hebrew expression "face to face" could have a figurative meaning. On the other hand, Ibn Ezra had long before provided the appropriate explanation for this expression in the Pentateuch: "without a mediator."[87] |316|

We already know that Spinoza is not wanting in shocking clarity. He explains the passage cited above as follows: "that is, just as two men ordinarily exchange thoughts through the medium of their two bodies."[88] God thus has a voice and a face, because He is a body. As a body He communicates with another body, just as one human being communicates with another. One may neither add nor subtract from the law revealed to Moses; but it never commanded "us to believe that God is incorporeal or that he has no form or figure, but only that he is God." [89] We may certainly call it sophistry when he adds that we are not to "assign any image to him or make any," as if the Decalogue prohibited only the making of an image involving false imputation, whereas there could be such a thing as a legitimate image of God. |317|

Now, however, we can finally understand what it means that only the existence of God is the object of natural faith, not a concept of God that involves knowledge. "But indeed, Scripture does clearly indicate that God has a form, and that when Moses heard God speaking, it befell him to see God, but to behold only back parts. So I have no doubt that here lies some mystery, which I shall discuss more fully later on."[90] However, he airs the mystery himself, and immediately.

Spinoza notes Moses' prominence among all the prophets of Israel, before and after him, with the phrase "whom the Lord knew face to face."[91] While he limits the face to the voice, "for not even Moses ever saw the Lord's face,"[92] he distinguishes here between the *mind* and the face and the rest of the body. "...He communicates his essence to our minds."[93] He adds: "without employing corporeal means."[94] One is supposed to think that God communicates with the human mind in general; but for that purpose physical means should not be rejected. What is meant here by the rejection of physical means? "Nevertheless, a man who can perceive *solely by the mind*[95] that which is *neither contained in the most basic principles of our knowledge* nor able to be deduced from them must need possess a mind whose excellence far *surpasses* the *human* mind."[96] Here again we must ask: If man seeks to know God solely through the mind, does he thus place himself outside the context of "the basic principles of our knowledge"? Does *ethics*, for example, lie outside this context?

|318| However, Spinoza continues: "Therefore I do not believe that anyone has attained such a degree of perfection surpassing all others, except Christ. To him God's ordinances leading men to salvation were received not by words or by visions, but directly, so that God manifested himself to the Apostles through the mind of Christ as he once did to Moses through an audible voice. The Voice of Christ can thus be called the Voice of God in the same way as that which Moses heard."[97]

Let us analyze this sentence. First of all, we now understand why knowledge of God had to dispense with being derived from "basic principles": human knowledge is to be surpassed by Christ. Now, we will not pass judgment on Spinoza's attempt to produce an idea of the significance of Christ that does justice to his piety towards Christ's teachings. Our present task is only to examine how he differentiates between Christ and Moses. Moses hears a Voice of God; God, however, does not reveal himself to Christ at all. Only God's *placita* [ordinances] are revealed to him, without intermediary. Yet, if God does not reveal himself to Christ at all, then the analogy with Moses comes to naught. And again, one may wonder: If God reveals to Christ only the ordinances that lead men to salvation, then these must also contain the essence of God, if the revelation to Christ is not supposed to be abridged. However, in the case of Christ, it is not revelation; the recipients of revelation are now the Apostles, to whom God reveals himself "through the mind of Christ." Thus, the function served by the voice in Moses' case is served by the mind in the case of Christ.

Nevertheless, this mind is not the theoretical mind of the human being. But what other meaning do we know or could we conceive? Thus, it does not in fact remain mind for long. Instead the mind of Christ changes at once into "the Voice of Christ," which then "can be called the Voice of God." If Spinoza had extended his sentence to say that the mind of Christ is the mind of God, this would have fit his train of thought. The only possible |319| way to understand why he converts the mind back into a voice is to say that it was his intent to merge the physical, that is, the *human*, with the mind of Christ.

This intention becomes explicit in what follows. "In that sense it can also be said that the Wisdom of God—that is, wisdom that is more than human—*took on human nature* in Christ, and that Christ was the way of salvation."[98] Now it is once again the wisdom of God, not God himself, that has taken on human nature in Christ. Why only wisdom, which, after all, could easily be understood in the limited sense of *logos*? If God, however, has revealed himself as wisdom in the mind of Christ, then the Apostles themselves must have a share in it, if the revelation of this mind is supposed to be accessible to them. Once again, it is the illusion of pantheism that makes such communication possible in the mind between God and man. Only thus can we understand Spinoza and do him justice. His pantheism predisposes him favorably toward the divinity of Christ, and his predisposition renders the divinity of Christ comprehensible.

It is clear from the sentence immediately following that, in making this confession, Spinoza is, so to speak, checking his own pulse: "But I must here ask it to be noted that I am certainly not alluding to the doctrines held by some Churches about Christ."[99] We must stop here: Only *some* churches hold different doctrines about Christ? To understand this claim, one has to consider that Spinoza probably knew of the doctrine of *Zwingli*, and that, in his circle at Rijnsburg,[100] he flattered himself with the illusion that the dogmatic conception of the Trinity had been universally overcome. To be sure, he was shy about presenting his pangs of conscience; he continues: "...nor am I denying them; for I freely confess that I do not understand them."[101] He eased his conscience in a similar way in his letters.[102] But he did |320| not ask himself the following: If, to put it more correctly, as distinct from the general views of the church and of religion, some more recent dogmatic reforms are compatible with pantheism, should not this compatibility also hold for the God who revealed himself to Moses? And it is all the more conspicuous that he did not consider this question here, since elsewhere, as we shall see, he traces his own pantheism to "some of the Hebrews."[103] With |321| this—his own—historical reflection, the entire distinction he has made here between Moses and Christ disintegrates.

The comparison concludes as follows: "Therefore, if Moses spoke with God face to face, as a man may do with his fellow (that is, through the medium of their two bodies), then Christ communed with God mind to mind."[104] The parenthetical remark reveals that the point is directed not so much against Moses as against his God: God has a body. However, the God who communes with Christ is only mind. But if the God of the Old Testament is only a body, one would have to think it absolutely impossible for Spinoza to conceive of the two Testaments as one, undivided work, for then all of prophecy would contain no mental or ethical conception of God. And if that purports to be his opinion, how could it then be possible, just by enhancing the value [of the one], to combine the two Testaments in one and the same work? Spinoza is aware of this objection when he undertakes a philological inquiry into the *mind of God* in the Old Testament.

It is inevitable that for this purpose he should cite passages in which the spirit of God and, no less, the divine spirit of man are clearly revealed. However, his philology lumps the spirit of the spirit and the spirit of the *wind* and other kinds of spirit all together in one basket. Finally, the *Holy Spirit*, or better, the *spirit of holiness*, makes its appearance as well. The prophets are alleged to have possessed the spirit of holiness by virtue of their *imaginative faculty*, so that this spirit of holiness can also be called the "spirit... of God,... and the prophets could be said to have possessed the mind of God."[105] Here *spirit* means only the faculty of representation and imagination. For the rest, all the expressions for spirit in the prophets |322| "mean merely this, that the prophets were endowed with an extraordinary *virtue*, exceeding the normal, and that they devoted themselves to *piety* with especial constancy."[106]

Thus the prophets possess only *ethical* spirit. *Is there then no connection between ethics and knowledge of God?* If, then, someone bases ethics on God, and if his ideas of God neither rise to the standard of knowledge nor contain any knowledge at all, for such a man would not genuine ethics have to be a miracle?

Another odd reason emerges for the distinctiveness accorded here to the prophets despite their intellectual insufficiency. Natural knowledge, which all human beings share with the prophets, is not "so highly prized, and particularly in the case of the Hebrews, who vaunted themselves above all men—indeed, despising all men, and consequently the sort of knowledge that is common to all men."[107] This is, then, the final reason for the distinctiveness of the prophets: the haughtiness of the Hebrews toward all men and their contempt for the knowledge[108] that is common to all. Is this some kind of historical judgment? Did Spinoza draw it somehow from Maimonides, from his predecessors and successors?

Finally, Spinoza accounts for the style of the prophets by invoking their lowly spiritual and mental state: "the perceptions and teachings of the prophets were nearly all in the form of parables and allegories, and why all spiritual matters were expressed in corporeal form..."[109] "We shall no longer wonder why Scripture, or the prophets, speak so strangely or obscurely of the Spirit, or mind, of God... why the Holy Spirit was seen by those with Christ as a dove descending, by the Apostles as tongues of flame, and by Paul at his conversion as a great light. All this is in full agreement with the common imagination of Gods and Spirits."[110] Thus here the Apostles are |323| grouped together, without any distinction, with the prophets, and in the preceding passages no distinction is made between the prophets and Moses.

One would think that in this chapter Spinoza had rendered final judgment on the spirit of the prophets. For at the end of the chapter, he raises the question of the *certainty* of prophetic knowledge. It would seem that the answer was given with the question itself. However, the question is dealt with further in the next chapter, "Of the Prophets."

Immediately we hear again: "...those who look to find understanding and knowledge of things natural and spiritual in the books of the Prophets go far astray."[111] Are we to suppose that all wisdom and knowledge of spiritual things, like knowledge of natural things, are absent in the prophets? What, then, would be the use of Scripture, and what would be its connection to religion? A qualification must follow. Prophecy does not possess the certainty of knowledge. "...The certainty afforded by prophecy was not a mathematical certainty, but only a moral certainty."[112] One would think this sufficient and correct; for religion is supposed to concern itself only with morality.

Thus, the authentic moral content of prophetic knowledge must be demoted, despite its moral certainty: "...the certainty of the prophets was based... lastly and most importantly, [on the consideration that] the minds of the prophets were directed exclusively toward what was right and good."[113] To be sure, such content is not yet enough. The question

|324| remains whether the prophets have expressed the entire content of religion. Only in that case do they actually have a relationship to religion. "[P]rophecy did not render the prophets more learned..."[114] To be sure, Spinoza does not make this claim with regard to "uprightness and morality."[115] But "their [the prophets'] teaching concerning the attributes of God was in no way singular. Their beliefs about God were very vulgar,[116] and their revelations were accommodated to these beliefs."[117] Nonetheless, they won praise "for piety and faithfulness."[118] Again, we have to ask: Do piety and faithfulness simply have no connection to cultured knowledge, especially knowledge of God and his attributes? Must it not be the case that vulgar notions of ethics will conform to vulgar notions of God?

The Spinoza does not tire of identifying these vulgar notions in Moses as well. It is instructive to observe how he shifts from deficient knowledge of God to accepted moral insight, but also from the latter back to the former. In Spinoza's view, for Moses, God is only eternal being, just as in Hebrew Jehovah "expresses these three tenses of the verb 'to be.' As for God's nature, Moses taught no more than that God is merciful, gracious, etc., and extremely jealous..."[119] This "etc." should be noted. All the other attributes of God, his *love and faithfulness*, are suppressed by means of this "etc.," except the attribute "extremely jealous." This is Spinoza's inaccurate translation of the thirteenth attribute, on which the Talmud and philosophers of religion have based the most important and also the most interesting insights into the essence of God.[120]

The only concession granted to Moses' conception of God is that he cannot be expressed through an image, "since Moses... has formed no image

|325| of God in his brain, and God... did not appear to Moses in the form of an image."[121] However, what is the meaning of the uniqueness of God if not to indicate the inadequacy of any image?

Although the uniqueness of God is accepted as an article of faith, and, as we have seen, on the basis of Scripture, the unbelievable occurs: Spinoza *denies* that Moses accepts the *unity* of God.

It is difficult to believe that such a conclusion could be drawn even from Spinoza's literal method of interpreting the text of the Bible. "Moses *did indeed concede that there were beings who... acted in God's place*; that is, beings to whom God gave the authority, right, and power to guide nations, to look after them and care for them. But he taught that this Being whom it was their duty to worship was the highest and supreme God, or (to use the Hebrew phrase) the God of Gods."[122] At the same time, Spinoza questions whether these deputies of God were also created by him, noting that Moses had nothing to say on the matter.

Among the passages adduced in support of this idea,[123] which incidentally contradicts the uniqueness of God as grounded in Scripture, one citation is especially instructive: II Chronicles 32:19. It is an account of Sennacherib's messengers and communications during the siege of Jerusalem. "They spoke of the *God of Jerusalem* as though He were like *the gods of the other peoples of the earth,* made *by human hands.*" Spinoza cites this verse in support of his view that the God of Israel is the *God of Jerusalem.*[124] He was unmoved by the immense gravity of this verse: they speak of the God of Jerusalem as they would of the gods of the other peoples of the earth, who are the work of human hands.

He sees here only the God of Jerusalem—and completes his circular argument: Moses "furthermore taught that this Being had reduced our visible world from chaos to order [...] and had given Nature its seeds. He therefore possesses supreme right and power over things, and [...] by virtue of this supreme right and power he had chosen the Hebrew nation for himself alone, together with a certain territory [...], leaving other nations and lands to the care of *other gods standing in his place.* For this reason he was called the God of Israel and the God of Jerusalem."[125] That is the reference from the book of Chronicles. Thus, this state of mind is the basis of the claim that Moses teaches that there is not just *one* God, but also many other gods beyond the one from Jerusalem. And yet, this unique God is supposed to be the God of faith, and this man Moses is supposed to have taught ethics, the sole content of religion!

|326|

Of course, Moses laid down a moral code only as a "lawgiver"—that is to say, by way of distinction, "not as a philosopher."[126] However, that can only mean: not as a moralist. And the precise point here is to question the value of this morality. "Therefore the right way of life, or true living, and the worship and *love* of God, were for them *bondage* rather than true freedom, the grace and gift of God..."[127] And this bondage is based on love!

Moses is probably the first among all religious thinkers to command that one love God, the first to raise the problem of God in relation to love. And love is supposed to be just bondage?

|327| To reach a judgment on this Bible critic's scientific disposition as a whole, it would be worthwhile to review all his other statements on this core principle, but one citation will suffice: "So we conclude that we must believe the prophets only with regard to the *purpose* and *substance* of the revelation."[128] Nonetheless, the purpose and substance of Scripture remain, as they have been from Cain onward, to "admonish... to live the true life."[129] Yet this true life can be found in Scripture, and thus in religion, only in a qualified way. Thus, what emerges here is the actual aim of the *Tractatus*: "the differentiation of philosophy from theology."[130] What is really meant is the separation of philosophy from religion.

The *third chapter* treats "Of the Vocation of the Hebrews, and whether the gift of prophecy was peculiar to them." Even the combination of questions is striking. Scripture speaks of the prophets of the nations; thus the difference can lie only in the value of prophecy itself. And it is the value of prophecy on which the election of Israel is based. Its peculiar value, however, has already been compromised, making it impossible for the vocation [of the Hebrews] to retain any sound ethical value.

Spinoza begins this more political section with a general discussion of the concept of natural laws, in which his pantheism is clearly audible. For Spinoza, the main task of reason is to have "taught us... to organize a *society* under fixed laws, and to concentrate the strength of all its members into one body, as it were, a social body."[131] The formation of the *state* is the most important step, according to "God's direction." God's direction is synonymous with *the natural order* or "chain of natural events."[132] The criterion for distinguishing between nations consists, therefore, in the structure of the state. "*Through this alone, then, do nations differ from one another, namely, in respect of the kind of society and laws...*"[133]

|328| To start, the *concept* of law employed here is questionable. Are the laws only *laws of the state*, or also laws of *faith*? Spinoza continues: "Thus the Hebrew nation was chosen by God before all others not by reason of its understanding or its spiritual qualities, but by reason of its social organization and good fortune..."[134] For Spinoza, it is clear from Scripture that "the Hebrews surpassed other nations in this alone, that they were *successful [feliciter]* in achieving security for themselves and overcame great dangers... In other respects they were no different from other nations, and God was equally gracious to all."[135] Spinoza then concludes that the Hebrews were no better than other nations not only intellectually, but also "in respect of virtue and the true life..."[136] In this respect, too, "very few of them" were "chosen."[137]

One would hope that at least in this one respect the prophets were chosen, and that the election of Israel consisted in this vocation of prophets. But Spinoza immediately continues: "*Therefore their election and vocation consisted only in the material success and prosperity of their state*; nor do we see that God *promised* anything other than this to the *patriarchs* or their successors. Indeed, in return for their obedience the Law promises them nothing other than the continuing *prosperity of their state* and material advantages."[138] At the very least, it is striking that Spinoza did not consider the promise to Abraham, "And *all the families of the earth* shall bless themselves by you,"[139] which is in no way limited to just the descendants of the patriarch. |329|

But it is especially striking that Spinoza condemns the promise of a state on the grounds that it serves an egoistic and utilitarian end, whereas he has just said that the establishment of a state is the *purpose* of the life of nations. Here the security of the state is viewed as a defect, a product of opportunism that is just one of life's rewards.

From the standpoint of critical biblical scholarship, the Israelite Bible and biblical law actually serve a twofold purpose. The first, to be sure, is the establishment of an Israelite state, entailing the collection and redaction of all the legends and stories of the individual tribes that are to be joined together in it. However, a second purpose is inherently linked with the first: alongside particularism and politics in general, to found and elaborate a *religion*, a religion in which national political particularism *must* be transformed into a *universalism of humanity*. Spinoza did not recognize this connection. While he did not entirely ignore the universalism of the prophets, its connection to the particularism that serves the establishment of a national state was not clear to him. This is why Spinoza, while recognizing the purpose of the state—and he does consider it necessary— could overlook the purpose of religion. At the same time, this concept of the state seeks to realize the purpose of religion, even by means of its prophetic political actors.

Yet it is simply impossible to understand how Spinoza could take the necessary particularism of the laws of the state and generalize it to apply to the *entire* content of the Mosaic and Old Testament laws. It is especially problematic that Spinoza extends this generalization from the five books of Moses to *all* the other books of the Old Testament, even though, as we will see, Spinoza himself cites other passages from the latter.

|330| Thus the end of these discussions meanders in contradictions and repetitions of the same theses, which are contradicted by the citations from the Prophets and Psalms. "But this I will add, that the laws contained in the Old Testament were revealed and ordained for the Jews *alone*."[140] The particular state requires particular laws. But are all the laws of the Old Testament limited solely to laws of the state? Does the Old Testament not contain some laws of universal human ethics? Spinoza does not ask this question. He does, however, raise petty, caviling objections from the sphere of general history and culture, supporting them with citations from the Bible.

On the other hand, he does not remember—does he really not remember?—that the Talmud invented and established the *Noahide laws*. Their purpose was, first, to ensure that all other nations were not excluded from divine law. But their purpose was also to preclude the possibility that biblical law should appear to be the *sole* ethical law. We will have more to say on this later.[141]

Spinoza cites the oracles of the prophets, such as Malachi 1:11—"I have no pleasure in you... For my name is great among the nations"[142]—as proof that "the Jews at that time were no more beloved of God than were other nations" and that the election of the Jews had as its purpose only "their temporal material prosperity."[143] Thus temporal felicity is now combined with corporeal felicity.

What, however, is the source of Spinoza's insight that God must love all nations? Now come the citations from the Psalms and Prophets. Certain verses from the Psalms must be particularly embarrassing for Spinoza: Psalms 145:18, and verse 9 in that psalm, but especially Psalms 33:15: "he fashioneth *[their] hearts alike*."[144] So it turns out that the one, unique God not only provided the Chaos, but also created the hearts of all humankind, even outside Palestine.

Other contradictions follow. In one place he writes: "...the Hebrews were concerned to record their own history, not that of other nations,"[145]
|331| but then directly thereafter: "that Hebrew prophets were sent by God not only to their own nation but to many others."[146] Thus he quotes Isaiah's and Jeremiah's moving expressions of international compassion for Egypt and Moab, and then adds Balaam's prophecy, to prove his great claim that "the other nations, like the Jews, also had their prophets, who prophesied to them and to the Jews."[147] A novelty emerges here as an aside: that heathen prophets prophesied for Israel, just as Israelite prophets did for

the heathen nations, and to their benefit. To be sure, Balaam masked his role well.

Finally, Spinoza also interprets Exodus 33:16, Moses' petition for divine protection for the existence of the nation, with the phrase "So shall we be separated, I and thy people, from all the people that are on the face of the earth."[148] He has the following to say about this *historical* recognition of religious distinction ("I and thy people"): "Surely it is absurd that Moses should begrudge God's presence to the Gentiles, or that he should have ventured to make such a petition to God."[149] According to Spinoza, Moses sought only God's special *external* help. "Therefore Moses is here concerned with the choosing of the Hebrews *only in the way I have explained*, and sought nothing else from God."[150] Thus, Moses understands his own distinctiveness, the distinctiveness of his nation and the election of Israel only as God's external aid.

Then Spinoza cites *Paul* as well, with his zeal against the law, to which Jews, like Gentiles, have been subject, and therefore subject to sin.[151] Paul concludes: "it was for all nations that God sent his Christ to free all men alike from the bondage of the law."[152] Now it is well known that Paul understood by law not only the ceremonial law, but also the *moral law.* |332| Thus, it cannot be entirely correct when the text goes on to say: "so that no longer would they act righteously from the law's command but from the unwavering resolution of the will. *Thus Paul's teaching coincides exactly with ours.*"[153] This would hold only if, for Paul, *faith* were synonymous with the "unwavering resolution of the will." The will per se, however, cannot rely on salvation through Christ; the will can only rely on faith in salvation.

At the end of the chapter, Spinoza cites warnings that challenge biblical guarantees of *Israel's eternal existence* and threaten the nation with destruction if it persists in its obstinacy. He construes these passages as direct prophecies. We will encounter more such examples of his understanding of the Bible. Here he also touches on the question of the *continued existence* of the Jews, long after the loss of the alleged object of their religion, their state. For this too he has an explanation: "As to their continued existence for so many years when scattered and stateless, this is in no way surprising, since they have separated themselves from other nations to such a degree as to incur the *hatred* of all, and this not only through external rites alien to the rites of other nations, but also through the mark of circumcision, which they most religiously observe. *That they are preserved largely through the hatred of other*

|333| *nations* is demonstrated by historical fact."[154] What follows are references to the devastating success of the *conversion of Jews* in Spain and Portugal!

Yet Spinoza holds circumcision in higher esteem than conversion. "The mark of circumcision, too, I consider to be such an important factor in this matter that I am convinced that this by itself will preserve their nation forever."[155] This, of course, contradicts the promise of their demise. However, Spinoza is not concerned about this contradiction. He pursues his preoccupation with this historical arcanum still further. "Indeed, were it not that the fundamental principles of their religion discourage manliness, I would not hesitate to believe that they will one day, given the opportunity—such is the mutability of human affairs—establish once more their independent state, and *that God will again choose them*."[156] Unless one assumes an element of diabolical irony, it is difficult to understand how the political view expressed by Spinoza here is compatible with his religious view regarding divine sovereignty over the world.

However, considering that Spinoza expresses this viewpoint frequently and in all seriousness, one might offer the following explanation: to be sure, he finds nothing, either in his fund of knowledge nor in his conscience, to challenge the position he takes on the historical mission of Israel. It could just be that his innate love for his own religious nation prevailed over his stubborn frame of mind, entangling him in self-contradiction against his will, however base his motivation.

Thus it would still remain the case that the religion of the Jews is appropriate only to their own state. However, Spinoza's attitude is revealed yet again when he compares circumcision with the "pigtail of the Chinese."[157] He prophesies that the Chinese too will regain their empire once the Tartars lose control. But he appropriately refrains from carrying this analogy any further.

|334| The *fourth chapter* is titled "Of the Divine Law." The chapter begins with definitions of the *concept of law* as it relates to *nature* and to *the human world*. In the latter meaning, law becomes a commandment for human conduct. Spinoza proceeds to distinguish between human and divine law. Human law serves "to safeguard life and the commonwealth."[158] Divine law, however, "is concerned only with the supreme good, that is, the true knowledge and love of God."[159] Now God becomes an object of *true knowledge*, while faith, of course, must forfeit any claim to true dogma. (See above p. 8) The supreme good, however, is to consist in endowing our intellect with the greatest perfection.

Now the entire arsenal of the *Ethics* is deployed, such as "without God nothing can be or be conceived,"[160] that "everything in Nature involves and expresses the concept [of God],"[161] and that "the greater our knowledge of natural phenomena, the more perfect our knowledge of God's essence."[162] Our supreme good "not merely depends on the knowledge of God but consists entirely therein." Our *blessedness* consists in the supreme good of knowledge. For this reason the means of attaining the blessedness of the supreme good can "be called God's commands."[163] Here too Spinoza's *pantheism* cannot be denied: "for they are ordained for us *by God himself, as it were, insofar as he exists in our minds.*" Thus, in the end, divine law is grounded in our mind. Yet this does not mean that our mind bears *responsibility* for producing and obeying the law. Instead, it means that, *by definition*, the human mind and God are *identical*, inasmuch as He exists in the human mind. |335|

Human laws have a different purpose, "as long as they have not been sanctioned by revelation..."[164] What does this mean? Are there revealed laws that are nevertheless human? This is possible only if they do not relate to the *supreme good*. And yet they are related to God? Now the qualification is understandable: "the sum of the divine law and its chief command"[165] is the supreme good; its "essential nature"[166] consists in the supreme good. But Spinoza does not immediately say what its non-essential contents are. He refers only to the *sensual* means that *sensual* man needs. After this definition of human law, which is also divine law, he states: "And in this sense the law of Moses, although it was not of universal application but specially adapted to the character and preservation of one particular people, can nevertheless be termed the Law of God, or divine law..."[167] Is this acknowledgment not a contradiction? The explanation follows: "since we believe it to have been sanctioned by prophetic insight."[168] Why do we believe this? To that question the anonymous author[169] gives no answer.

In the content of the "natural divine law"[170] Spinoza then distinguishes between *laws possessing universal validity* and *historical narratives*. Belief in the latter is not required. Finally, he also segregates *ceremonies*, "actions that are in themselves indifferent," that only "symbolize," and "whose explanation surpasses human understanding."[171] As a fourth point he cites the principle "the supreme reward of the divine law is the law itself."[172] Here he has incorporated, verbatim, a saying from the Mishna, from the well-known Sayings of the Fathers, adding only the word "supreme": "The reward of duty is duty."[173] But he does not want, after all, to be indebted to the Pharisees. |336|

The four parts of the content of the law are then considered separately. The first question concerns the possibility of [conceiving of] God, as lawgiver, from the standpoint of the natural light [of reason]. For since God not only exists in *our* minds but is synonymous with *nature in its entirety* and in its necessity, an incongruity arises between *necessary* being and commanded being. Hence, the command, or the law, being only part of the phenomenon, must be wanting. Accordingly, God "revealed to Adam only the punishment he must incur if he should eat of that tree; the necessary entailment of that punishment was not revealed. Consequently, Adam perceived this revelation not as an eternal and necessary truth but as a law, that is to say, an enactment from which good or ill consequence would ensue..."[174]

Thus Adam was just inadequately informed by God. "For this same reason, that is, their lack of knowledge, in relation to the Hebrews alone the Decalogue was a law... But if God had spoken to them directly, employing no physical means, they would have perceived this not as a law, but as an eternal truth. What we are here saying about the Israelites and Adam also applies to the prophets... For example, in the case of Moses too..."[175] What is the purpose of this distinction between immediate revelation and that which employs physical means? We know the purpose already.

|337|

This inadequate revelation applies "only to the prophets [...] but not to Christ. With regard to Christ, although he also appears to have laid down laws in God's name, we must maintain that he perceived things truly and adequately; for Christ was not so much a prophet as the mouthpiece of God. It was through the mind of Christ... that God made revelations to mankind..."[176] By distinguishing between the revelation of Christ and the revelation of the prophets, Spinoza aims to make a distinction between the *principal content* of the divine law, consisting of eternal truths, and the *statutes* and *practices* ordained by Moses.

As we have already discussed, it is difficult to fathom how this distinction could be based on that between *what is mediated or indirect and what is immediate or direct.*[177] After all, it is not immediacy if the *one, unique* God is *also* Christ *at the same time.* But aside from this, and aside from the particular question of the physicality of this mediation, the second question is of current importance for all culture: if one concedes that Christ is the mouthpiece of God, how can one also say he had *adequate knowledge*? This would mean he was a *philosopher.*

Apparently, Spinoza has once again abandoned the *methodological* distinction between religion and philosophy, although his main purpose was to separate theology from philosophy. His indecisiveness on this fundamental question is reflected in the indecisiveness of his terminology: "...God revealed himself to *Christ, or to Christ's mind*, directly,[178] and not through words and images, as in the case of the prophets... For it is when a thing is perceived by *pure* thought, without words or images, that it is understood."[179] However, if God revealed himself only to the *mind* of Christ, and if this is supposed to have occurred without words, why is Christ still called the mouthpiece of God? Is not a mouth required essentially because of words?

|338|

Furthermore, if he is the mouthpiece, is he not then God himself, if it is at all true that, in the word of God, God exists for man? And why is it stated here yet again: "Therefore in this matter he acted in God's place, adapting himself to the character of the people"[180]—that is, through the use of parables. "But doubtless, to those to whom it was granted to know the mysteries of Heaven, his teaching took the form of eternal truths, not of prescribed laws. In this way he freed them from bondage to the law, while nevertheless giving further strength and stability to the law..."[181] The last sentence makes us doubtful. It would seem, after all, that bondage to the law is incompatible with the preservation of the law, to say nothing of strengthening it. Indeed, this claim is made here only with reference to the *parables*.

On the *second* question, which concerns *natural light* in the Bible, only Hebrew sources are taken into consideration, particularly the wise Solomon in Proverbs, followed by the Prophets. "All this is plainly in accord with natural knowledge, for it is natural knowledge that teaches us ethics and true virtue, once we have tasted the excellence of knowledge."[182] But here too the ambiguity persists in the relationship between this [kind of] natural knowledge and the knowledge of philosophy.

|339|

The *fifth chapter* treats *ceremonies*. It is argued that they relate only to the physical, temporal happiness of the Hebrews and to the protection of their commonwealth. As divine laws they are based solely on revelation. But how is revelation justified in this context? Spinoza does not ask. He justifies himself instead *by citing passages from Scripture*. Now one would think that here only Christ, only the Gospels, would have the floor, as the unmediated word of God. Quite to the contrary, Spinoza cites almost exclusively the Prophets and Psalms. But do they not also belong to the Old Testament, even if he were to say what he does not say: that they contradict the law of Moses? *Thus, he leaves it to the prophetic polemics against sacrifice to take up the case against ceremonial rites.*

This series of quotations is interrupted when he confronts the "five books commonly attributed to Moses"[183]—in character for Spinoza, as if our question were stirring in him too. "And although these five books contain *much about moral teaching* as well as ceremonial observance, these passages are put forth *not* as moral teaching of universal application to *all* men, but as commands... that have regard only for the utility of the commonwealth.[184] For example, it is not as a teacher or prophet that Moses forbids the Jews to kill or steal; it is as a lawgiver or ruler that he issues these commands. He does not *justify* his precepts by *reasoning*... So, too, his command not to commit adultery refers only to the good of the commonwealth and state. If he had intended this to be a moral precept... he would have condemned not merely the external act but *the very wish (consensus animi)*, as did Christ."[185] *Consensus animi* is a Stoic term that signifies the spiritualization of *all* acts of consciousness by virtue of *being accompanied* by *consensus animi*. It goes without saying that this kind of spiritual supervision by consciousness is assumed in any *legal* act. As a consequence, the role of consciousness does not bring about any *moral* difference.

|340|

Concerning *reward*, however, for Moses reward is material, whereas for Christ it is supposed to be spiritual. In actuality, this difference can be based only on the law of the respective state or on universal law. Meanwhile, it may be said that the Decalogue has at least begun to prove its universality in the history of humankind.

After this interpolation, the citations continue, passages from the Prophets directed against ceremonial rites. To be sure, it is troubling straightaway that the first ceremony to be mentioned is the *Sabbath*,[186] in that marvelous chapter 58 of the book of Isaiah. The man has no clue of the *significance of the Sabbath for love and justice*, initially for the state, but also, in what follows, for all the nations and states of the world. That is to say, he does not recognize the connection between ceremony and social love and justice. *For the Sabbath is the epitome of all social laws and all liturgical ceremonies in Israel.*[187] Thus, when Spinoza goes on to say that "the Hebrews are not bound to practice their ceremonial rites, since the destruction of their state is clear from Jeremiah" (i.e., 9:23),[188] he ignores the fact that Jeremiah acknowledged the social significance of the Sabbath for all posterity (17:21).

The statements that follow involve judgments on the *New* Testament, which allegedly "teaches only moral doctrine,"[189] on the Apostles, "who abolished ceremonial rites,"[190] and on the Pharisees, who "did indeed retain these rites, or a great part of them...; but their object in so doing was to oppose the Christians rather than to please God."[191] The historical idea |341| that both [ceremony and moral doctrine] may have interacted to form the historical basis of the Pharisees does not occur to Spinoza. Instead he follows with the very odd remark that as early as after the destruction of the *First* Temple ceremonial rites were discontinued. This can only be understood as a reference to sacrifices. Yet Spinoza says: "They turned their backs on the entire Mosaic Law... Therefore there is no doubt that, since the fall of their independent state, Jews are no more bound by the Mosaic Law than they were before their political state came into being."[192] What follows is a strange observation on sacrifices during the age of the *patriarchs* and the like.

To place the actual meaning of ceremony beyond all doubt, Spinoza engages once again in general observations on the *origin of the state*, proceeding from there to the *Hebrew state*. According to Spinoza, Moses intended to educate the people to fulfill their duty not out of *fear*. This was his reason for introducing *religion* into the state. Nonetheless, he demanded that the people be "utterly subservient"[193] and give *constant* thought to the law.[194] To this end the most diverse commandments are now intermingled, without any distinction regarding their *purpose*. It is merely stated repeatedly that they all have a single purpose, that "men [...] should at all times acknowledge that they were... completely subservient to another. From all these considerations it is quite indisputable that ceremonial observances contribute nothing to blessedness, and that those specified in the Old Testament, and indeed the whole Mosaic Law, were relevant... to no more than *physical* advantages."[195] Before the sentence stating that the purpose of ceremony is that men should always be "only under the rule of |342| another," as in Gebhardt's translation,[196] the wording of the text requires closer attention.

The text reads: "This, then, was the object of ceremonial observance, that men should never act of their own volition, but always at *another's* behest, and that in their actions and inward thought they should at all times acknowledge that they were not their own masters, but completely subordinate to *another*." But who is the "other" under whose command and law men thus place themselves? It cannot, after all, be Moses, for he is only the servant of God and never purports to be the Lord. *Therefore God is this other!*

That is the dreadful conclusion to which this critique of ceremony leads. And it is clear from what follows that this conclusion is intentional. For Spinoza could not avoid the question of the status of ceremonial rites in the *New* Testament. "With regard to Christian ceremonies, namely, baptism, the Lord's Supper, festivals, public prayers and all the other ceremonies that are, and always have been, common to all Christendom, if they were ever instituted by Christ or the Apostles (of which I am not yet convinced), they were instituted only as external symbols of a universal church, not as conducing to blessedness or as containing an intrinsic holiness."[197]

In judging this position, one must especially keep in mind the illusions that Spinoza sought to maintain in relation to his Christian friends. To be sure, he was disabused of these illusions, to his great disappointment, so much so that these disputes led to a complete break with most of his friends, even with Oldenburg.[198]

Furthermore, one may also consider that Spinoza may have been aware |343| of Zwingli's views, which he was rapidly approaching in his own desire for a more open conception of Christian worship.[199] Nevertheless, it is difficult to understand how he could declare baptism and communion to be external symbols, just because according to an old view they are signs of the *universal* church, that is, of the *catholicity* of faith. It is also difficult to understand how he could deny that these *sacraments* are related to *blessedness*.

For when he attacks Pharisaic Judaism against the background of the Prophets and Psalms, he should, after all, include all of ecclesiastical Christianity, on account of its blood-soaked conception of baptism and Holy Communion as ceremonies of unconditional dogmatic value. In Spinoza's time, the doctrine of Holy Communion, involving *transubstantiation*, also influenced the philosophy of substance. Moreover, the Thirty Years' War had just come to an end. Still, these issues are supposed to be merely external signs of the universal church, even though they had just caused such division.

As a genuine publicist, Spinoza draws his proof for this peculiar statement from the most recent press. In the Japanese empire, it was reported, the Christian religion is forbidden, and "the Dutch living there must refrain, by decree of the East India Company, from any public worship."[200] It is obvious that this exceptional case proves nothing about the general significance of baptism. There are similar legal exceptions in the case of circumcision. But this notice in the newspaper caused a great scandal. It was taken as a denunciation that exposed the anti-clerical and irreligious character of Dutch colonization. By citing this far-fetched rationale, Spinoza certainly did not show himself to be a circumspect politician of his party.

Further on, Spinoza considers the value, for faith, of biblical history, concluding that it was intended only for the "common people,"[201] in which it is "most effective in instilling obedience and devotion."[202] The narratives |344| do not form part of the *divine* law and hence also do not form part of blessedness. "Therefore if a man reads the narratives of Holy Scripture and has complete faith in them, yet pays no heed to the lesson that Scripture thereby aims to convey, and leads no better life, he might just as well have read the Koran or a poetic drama or at any rate ordinary history, giving the same attention as common people do to such writings."[203] Again, what is missing here is the main point that Spinoza himself had in mind: what *utility* these narratives have for the improvement of life, and whether, in this respect, poetic drama is their equal.

In general, it is remarkable that Spinoza, the Enlightenment politician, is unable to perceive or appreciate the social spirit contained in the Mosaic political constitution, which has proven to be so fruitful throughout the ages. Likewise, he cannot appreciate the anti-clerical and anti-aristocratic politics of the prophets, which are rooted in socialism. English Puritanism should have taught him better. However, his political formalism is in keeping with his publicistic bias. He is so consumed by this bias that not even his *Ethics* enables him to see beyond it. To live according to reason! That is his motto. And that is his sole ideal; its relative realization is the aim of his political ideas. The *church* must be challenged as a state within the state. Its historical origin lies in the theocracy of *ancient Judaism*. For this reason, the Bible, in which church and state are identical, must be challenged. This, in light of his *definitions*, is what Spinoza regards as the problem of human culture. He does not see that the religious and political affairs of the past were of a different kind, and that ancient religious texts must therefore be judged entirely differently. And the Bible is no different from Judaism as a whole. In ancient Israel the priests ruled; later it was the ceremonial law. Measured against the |345| true life, Judaism has no right to live.

Given such a central defect in his understanding of Judaism, it is now hardly astonishing that he was oblivious to *a central objection* that calls his entire theory into question. *The concept of the Noahide represents a critical argument against his theory.*

Of course, Spinoza is in thrall to the idea that all of Jewish teaching from Moses onward is not a religion at all, because it does not contain a universal natural morality. Hence, it is just a collection of laws for the Jewish state. However, rabbinic Judaism invented and developed the concept of *an adherent of natural religion*. The "*son of Noah*" (בן נח) is nothing more and nothing less.

Elsewhere in *natural law*, whether ancient or modern, there is only the *concept* of such a law. Of course, in international law of the late Roman period the concept was put into political practice. However, it was in rabbinic theology, as it concerns the Jewish state, that the personal value of the follower of natural religion emerged and was fully developed in case law. This fundamental concept of natural law, a talmudic doctrine, resulted neither from philosophical theory nor from international law as occasioned by the expansion of *Roman civil law*. Rather, it was a genetic development of the *concept of man* in Jewish monotheism. From the very beginning, the *stranger* is a central figure in the problem of religion. "There shall be *one* Torah for you, for the citizen and for the stranger who dwells among you" (Exodus 12:49).²⁰⁴ Here *Torah* means quite literally "the *law* and the *right* of the state." Thus, this ancient law concerning the stranger had already broken with the particularism of the ancient Jewish state. The God of the prophets ran in the blood of the God of Moses; the seed of messianic humanity was contained in [the law establishing] the civil equality of the stranger. The Talmud developed the stranger into the son of Noah.²⁰⁵

First, let us consider this new concept from the standpoint of *natural religion*. This new concept represents a position that is contrary to *revelation*. Revelation came first to the Israelites alone, and from them it was to be communicated to the nations of the earth. The son of Noah presents himself, therefore, as a corrective to this concept of revelation. Revelation occurred first not at Sinai, for God revealed himself to Noah before Sinai, and even Moses himself promulgated this revelation after the fact. This is a great and profound idea, testifying to an unambiguous universal humanism. The religious man was not born with Moses; he has been present since Noah. This natural religion was established by the true God himself.

Thus, teachers of natural law in modern times have been very enthusiastic about this concept. In *England* it was especially John Selden;²⁰⁶ in the Netherlands, Hugo Grotius. It is only Spinoza, with his rabbinic erudition, who does not realize that the *seven commandments of the sons of Noah* entail an absolute contradiction to his entire edifice. (Aside from

|346|

the prohibition of *idolatry*, which was, in any event, linked to immoral practices, and aside from the prohibition of *blasphemy* in Jewish territory, these commandments include *only ethical rules*, such as the prohibition of *murder*, of *incest*, of *theft*, and of eating a *limb* from a living animal, and, at the top of the list, the *establishment of a legal system*!) That Spinoza ignores all this is simply a psychological enigma.

And it would remain just an enigma, if it could not be resolved in another way. For after the sentence we encountered above, in which Spinoza demonstrates the gap that separates biblical narratives from attitudes concerning the true way of life, he suddenly says: "Now the Jews take a completely contrary view. They maintain that true beliefs and a true way of life contribute nothing to blessedness as long as men embrace them only from the natural light of reason, and not as teachings revealed to Moses by prophetic inspiration. This is what Maimonides ventures openly to affirm..."[207] Next he quotes the passage from Maimonides' *Code* in the Hebrew original followed by a Latin translation. It reads: |347|

כל המקבל שבע מצות ונזהר לעשותן הרי זה מחסידי אומות העולם ויש לו חלק לעולם הבא: והוא שיקבל אותן ויעשה אותן מפני שצוה בהן הקדוש ברוך הוא בתורה והודיענו על ידי משה רבינו שבני נח מקודם נצטוו בהן אבל אם עשאן מפני הכרע הדעת אין זה גר תושב ואינו מחסידי אומות העולם ואינו מחכמיהם.

(Anyone who accepts the seven commandments and observes them conscientiously belongs to the pious of the nations of the world and has a share in eternal life; as long as he accepts and observes them because God commanded them in the Torah and made it known to us through our teacher Moses that the sons of Noah of old [i.e., before the revelation] were obligated to follow them. But he who observes them only by a decision of his reason is not a resident sojourner and belongs neither to the pious of the nations of the world, nor to their sages.)[208]

First and foremost, it should be noted here that the passage cited is *not the only* one in Maimonides' *Code* that deals with this issue. There are two others. The first is in Laws of Repentance 3:5:[209]

וכן חסידי א"ה יש להם חלק לעה"ב.

(And likewise [i.e., like Israel] the pious of the nations of the world have a share in eternal life.)[210]

The second is in Laws of Testimony 11:10. In neither passage does one find either the qualification above or any other.

Furthermore, Joël[211] has already objected that Spinoza made use here of an incorrect variant reading. Joël points out that another variant omits not the predicate "a *sage* of the nations of the world," as is the case here, but only "the *pious* of the nations of the world."[212] The commentary printed on every page alongside the text of the *Code*, which no reader can overlook and to which every reader customarily takes recourse, indicates that this variant is correct.

|348| Moreover, this commentary explains that Maimonides' opinion is that of an individual and has no warrant in the sources.[213]

Van Vloten and Land corrected the passage in the text accordingly. Suppl. p. 146.[214]

First of all, it is clear that Spinoza was in fact given a reminder about an idea that is familiar to any literate Jew and that topples his entire theory. Yet instead of revising it, he seeks to undermine this venerable pillar of rabbinic Judaism. Thus, fortified by a defective variant reading, he cites *one* passage in Maimonides' *Code* to shake the authority of rabbinic Judaism. The citation proves that he had the Noahide in mind, but that he thought he could reduce him to naught by invoking Maimonides, a single late Jewish authority, however renowned, and, what is more, by giving an incomplete review of the Maimonidean evidence.

To refute this erroneous conclusion, however, we will follow Spinoza himself, relying first on the authority of the great teacher Maimonides. We therefore ask: How is it possible that Maimonides *himself* would have decided to qualify this passage? His decision would seem not only to rob the fundamental concept of the Noahide of its significance for natural law, but also, in *this* passage, to *contradict his own position*. The passage is, as mentioned, only one of *three* in which Maimonides attributes blessedness to the Noahide. *And in the other two passages this attribution is unconditional*, without the qualification that occurs only in this single, *third* instance.

We will no longer bother to question how Spinoza, considering his mastery of the sources, could have passed over two passages and cited only the one in order to exploit it for his purposes. We will not question Spinoza any further on this line of thinking and inquiry. We will ask our honest champion of religious rationalism[215] how, in this one passage, he could have deviated from the fundamental idea for which, in two other passages, he gave a formulation that has been of decisive and epochal significance for the subsequent development of Judaism.

We can find an explanation for this deviation in the context of the three |349|
passages, at least for the purpose of settling this question with regard to
Maimonides. In the two latter passages what is at issue is only the general
religious concept of the Noahide. Maimonides decided in favor of the general
concept, drawing on the discussion in the Talmud (Sanhedrin 105a)[216] in
which one of the two talmudic teachers reaches the same decision. In those
two passages, therefore, the issue is solely the weighty religious problem
of whether *blessedness* can be attributed to the Noahide, as it is to the
Israelite. It is Maimonides' great accomplishment that he elaborated this
talmudic idea, taking into account the view expressed in other passages [of
the Talmud], into a definitive decision: *blessedness is not dependent on faith
and the observance of the law of Moses.* Whoever simply acknowledges and
follows the *universal commandments of natural morality* also has share in
blessedness.

In the third passage, however, the issue is not, as above, the moral
legitimation of the Noahide, but *the resident sojourner*[217] and his right as an
inhabitant of a Jewish country. The text states explicitly: "in every place."[218]
In the two other passages, in the chapter on repentance and atonement[219]
and in the chapter on testimony,[220] Maimonides invoked his authority
as rabbinic judge. Here, on the other hand, he has to qualify his theory
in order to prevent its total collapse. For here the question concerns the
constitutional principle inherent in the idea of the *resident sojourner.* Thus,
it no longer concerns the theory of *natural law* expressed in a religious
sense in the right to *blessedness*; instead, it is a question of *constitutional
civil law* in historical context.

The question still remains, whether this qualification does not, in spite
of everything, annul Maimonides' theory in the end.

To counter such an argument, one must bear in mind that the Noahide
and the resident sojourner need not be absolutely identical, for the sole
reason that the Noahide is a theoretical concept, whereas the resident
sojourner is a political one. However, in the ancient world, the ethical rules
of the Noahide—rules such as those against *incest* and *idolatry* itself—were |350|
subject to a kind of *relativity.* For rules such as those just specified, often
an embellishing rationale was sought. As a *teacher of constitutional law,*
Maimonides had to carry out all this casuistry in his codification of the
Talmud, but *only as pure theory* that could no longer have any practical
application in his own time. His religious liberalism aroused in him strong
political and legal reservations.

Thus, one possible explanation is that he devised this qualification to appease himself—for it is, as we now acknowledge, in fact of his own devising—in order not to surrender the theoretical right and moral substance of the Jewish state to the sin of idolatry and incest. Accordingly, the Noahide who aspires to the status of resident sojourner should first provide assurance that he is not taking the seven commandments upon himself on the basis of his free reason. Faced with the relative validity of these ethical ideas, this Noahide might arrive at decisions that vary from day to day. He must pledge that he accepts these commandments as the Jewish law of the land. Only then will the Jewish state, which of course cannot be understood simply as an asylum for freethinkers, be protected in its moral substance against upheavals. In the "Maimonidean annotations" on this passage we read: "Whoever accepts the Noahide commandments as a *resident sojourner.*"[221] Thus Maimonides himself stresses the difference.

And now one must also consider that to *accept* the seven commandments in this form as divine command in no way entails *belief* in divine command. For in that case the seven commandments would have become at least eight. To accept them means accepting not an article of faith, but a political obligation. It is conceivable that the resident sojourner would enclose the formula in quotation marks. He might think, "This may be the belief of the Israelites, but I will accept the content of this belief, and this rationale for it, only as a practical duty. I commit to the law and to this rationale, so I am not permitted to make obedience to the law dependent on some other rationale." At issue, however, is only obedience to the law, not belief in the rationale for the law itself.

|351| Once again, however, we should note that this conclusion, even with the qualifying assumption, marks a great step forward in the progress of religious enlightenment. The non-Israelite need only assume the obligations of the seven commandments in order to acquire the rights of full citizenship as an Israelite. Moreover, he should also, according to Maimonides' *lone* opinion, acknowledge that Jews assume that their God granted him these rights through Moses. He should not be satisfied with the rationale that these commandments, the number of which varies, are based only on free reason.

However, if we set aside all political considerations, the Jewish idea, in its theoretical universality, assumes that *Moses' teaching was already judged to represent reason.* The sojourner need not believe this, but for Judaism, the idea has fundamental authority: *Moses was concerned not just with the* nation of Israel, but with all the nations, both before and after Noah. The nations, though they are not children of Israel, are understood to be sons of Noah. As such they have a share in blessedness, which is the expression of religious equality.

By citing only *one* of the *three* passages in Maimonides, Spinoza has not just allowed us to peer into his soul. More than that, this omission will be recognized for all time as the bulwark on which Spinoza's entire historical, political, and religious theory of the Jewish state and Judaism disintegrates in self-contradiction.

The *sixth chapter*, "Of Miracles," requires no closer analysis. For God is identical to nature. The laws of nature are thus his will and his order, which is therefore "fixed and immutable." The laws of nature are "so perfect... that nothing can be added or taken away from them." This understanding of the laws of nature, however, is only metaphorical; it does not reflect their logical character. Miracles therefore must be explained as "natural occurrences."[222]

The *seventh chapter* is titled "*Of the Interpretation of Scripture.*" Here |352| too Spinoza's pantheistic concept of nature is the guiding principle. "...The method of interpreting Scripture is no different from the method of interpreting Nature, and is in fact in complete accord with it."[223] The influence of *Bacon* comes into play here, more than that of *Descartes*. "For the method of interpreting nature consists essentially in composing a detailed *study of nature* from which... we can deduce the *definitions* of the things of nature. Now in exactly the same way the task of scriptural interpretation requires us to make a straightforward study of Scripture, and from this, as the source of our fixed data and principles, to deduce... the meaning of the authors..."[224] In this sense he seeks to interpret Scripture *based solely on Scripture itself.*

He also brings this principle to bear on moral doctrines. "...Although these themselves can be demonstrated by accepted axioms, it cannot be proved from such axioms that Scripture teaches these doctrines: this can be established only through Scripture itself."[225]

As for the *study of Scripture*, its chief topic is the language in which the books of Scripture are written.

Even the books of the New Testament are "Hebrew in character."[226] Furthermore, the statements made in each book must be assembled and classified. This is again plainly *Baconian* induction at work. The meaning "must be sought simply from linguistic usage,"[227] and in no wise from reason itself. He cites as an example the idea that God is *fire*, or he is *jealous*. Since |353| Moses "nowhere tells us that God is without passions or emotions, we must evidently conclude that Moses believed this, or at least that he intended to teach this, however strongly we may be convinced that this opinion is contrary to reason."[228] In this way Scripture is interpreted such that it contradicts monotheism.

Nevertheless, later, as soon as Scripture has ostensibly been made clear from Scripture itself, "the meaning of the prophets" can and should be examined—as if "the meaning of the prophets" had not already been prejudiced by the preceding methodological inquiry. Once it has been established that God is not free of passions, then it will hardly be possible to establish the meaning of the prophets. Nonetheless, universals are still established by analogy to the universals of nature. Spinoza again distinguishes between the *existence* of the One God and his providence: These "and similar matters, Scripture does not teach formally, or as eternal doctrine."[229] Scripture is thus stripped of its actual meaning and content.

After citing further examples, Spinoza moves on to the criticism of *opposing points of view*. It is again Maimonides in particular who is singled out as his adversary. Maimonides grants *reason* authority over the interpretation of Scripture. And now Spinoza cites the memorable example in which Maimonides, without any reservation, takes his rationalistic method of scriptural interpretation to its extreme conclusion: the biblical doctrine of creation. In the passage in question, Maimonides declares that creation contradicts reason just as much as do those passages that attribute corporeality to God. The latter, however, can be resolved by reason. "But the eternity of the world has not been proved; so |354| it is not necessary to do violence to the scriptural texts..."[230] This is what Maimonides would say. Accordingly, he also would have reinterpreted creation as eternity if *Aristotle* had demonstrated the eternity of the world. Spinoza seeks to check such excesses of rationalist absolutism by means of the "common natural light,"[231] which means, actually, through reason. Thus it still constitutes a norm more concrete than Scripture itself is purported to be.

It is interesting to see how Spinoza, faced with this philosophical endeavor, issues a call to arms *against philosophy*. According to the method above, the common people "would have to rely solely on the authority and testimony of *philosophy*[232] for their understanding of Scripture... This would indeed be a novel form of ecclesiastical authority, and a novel kind of priests or pontiffs..."[233] Yet these pontiffs are the philosophers; are they really identical?

It does not truly serve to promote the *Enlightenment* if philosophy is separated from theology by this kind of reasoning, by means of this method. For philosophy is also severed from philology. Moreover, morality, the principal content of Scripture, is recognized only as a set of edifying, ambiguous precepts, and what is worst of all, a barrier is erected between philosophy and "the natural capacity for thought that is universal among human beings,"[234] that is, in the *vulgus*.[235] Thus the barrier also separates philosophy and *natural religion*, even though natural religion contains eternal truths only inasmuch as they are verified, as a whole and in each detail, by philosophy.

The next *three chapters* are devoted to the criticism of the Old Testament, followed by *chapter 11*, which contains a brief critique of the Apostles and their epistles.

One important result of Spinoza's Bible criticism, insofar as he judges Scripture not as a work of literature, but as the word of God, is stated in the sentence "This much I can say with certainty, that in the matter of *moral* |355| *doctrines* I have never observed a fault or variant reading that could give rise to obscurity or doubt in such teaching." [236] One has to acknowledge that it is a sign of Spinoza's dominant interest in the faith of natural religion that he does not completely drown in the material from his thorough investigation of sources. In this instance, at least, he keeps his eyes fixed on the principal content of Scripture.

In the chapter on the Apostles, his objectivity is diminished once again. The additions and contradictions alone give him away. Here he says of the prophets: they were "called to preach and prophesy only to *certain* nations, not to *all* nations."[237] Still, he does not state that they were sent only for Israel. The epistles of the Apostles, however, he attributes not to revelation, but to natural light. They therefore contain pure morality.[238] What, however, is the relationship between this morality and the story of the life of Jesus in the Gospels? "Furthermore, does not religion as preached by the Apostles— who simply related the history of Christ—fall within the scope of reason?"[239] Does this assertion, which is based on revelation, contradict the assertion based on reason?

But the sentence continues: "yet its substance, which consists essentially in moral teachings, as does the whole of Christ's doctrine, can be readily grasped by everyone by the natural light of reason."[240] Spinoza is thus endeavoring to distinguish between the "simple narration of the history of Christ" and the "substance," which, like "the whole of Christ's doctrine," |356|

constitutes morality. The latter is subsumed within the natural light. Does he maintain that this assertion applies to the entire doctrine of Christ? The note limits this claim to the Sermon on the Mount.[241]

And in *chapter 12*, on "Scripture as the Word of God,"[242] we find a further noteworthy revision of the distinction between the two Testaments. For there it is stated that the Apostles "preached religion to all men as a universal law solely by virtue of Christ's passion."[243] The argument for universality is based on Christ's passion, but is thus inevitably limited, for all human beings, to those who believe in the passion.

Still, it is worth taking note of *the basis given here for the distinction between the two Testaments*—quite aside from the obligation to be fair in one's criticism, but just for the sake of objectivity. "The books of the New Testament contained *no* different doctrine, nor were they written as documents of a covenant, nor was the *universal* religion—which is *entirely in accord with Nature*—anything *new*, except in relation to men who knew it not."[244] But how can this statement, that there is no difference in doctrine between the Old and New Testaments, be compatible with the basic idea that the doctrine of the Old Testament is constitutional law, and that universal morality is the doctrine of the New? Does this supposed distinction imply no material difference?

All these prevarications, contradictions, qualifications, retractions, and reservations are the unmistakable symptoms of the author's unfulfilled ambition. Further on he says explicitly that the doctrine of *charity* "is everywhere commended in the highest degree in both Testaments."[245] Here, then, the difference between the two Testaments is erased by the central doctrine of charity. However, for the Bible critic the question remains, a question that is both personal and political: what is the relationship, as documented in the literature of both Testaments, between charity and *justice*?

|357|

The chapters that follow were covered in the context of the concept of religion and its relationship to reason, and likewise the chapter thereafter, on state and law. Just a few sentences from *chapter 17*, "The Hebrew State," deserve attention.

Initially, Spinoza concludes from theocracy that "the enemies of this state were the enemies of God."[246] A further conclusion concerns the relationship of *Jewish patriotism* to *piety. They were identical.* Piety, "together with *hatred for other nations, was so fostered and nourished by their daily ritual that it* [...] *became part of their nature...* Hence this daily invective, as it were, was bound to engender a *lasting hatred* of a most *deep-rooted kind*, since it was a hatred that... was believed to be a religious duty—for that is the bitterest and most persistent of all kinds of hatred." Hence, for Spinoza, the hatred of the nations was just a "reciprocation."[247] And according to Spinoza the strength with which the Hebrews promoted their fatherland follows from this hatred in turn. We will pass over the question of whether hatred as understood here, as a positive factor, can be reconciled with Spinoza's doctrine of the emotions.[248]

However, it is worth noting that Spinoza abruptly acknowledges that this state possesses *social* merit. The citizens of the state "had an equal share with the captain in lands and fields, and were each the owners of their share in perpetuity."[249] Thus, Spinoza highlights those laws that are directed *against poverty*; yet in this case his guiding political principle disguises the view that one's neighbor was only one's "fellow citizen."[250] Other agrarian social laws are reduced to the status of ceremonies. Even the *Sabbath* is buried among the ceremonies.

|358|

In *chapter 18*, political principles are deduced from the constitution and history of the Hebrews. *Here the connection that links this biblical inquiry with Spinoza's political and publicistic bias is exposed.* In a theocracy it is evident "how dangerous it is to refer to religious jurisdiction matters that are purely philosophical."[251] Moreover, Spinoza cautions against *setting up a monarchy*, adding the observation that the *removal* of a monarch is not only dangerous and unjust, but also useless. He cites recent examples in support of his claim.

Chapter 19 presents the positive principle *that religion and worship are subject to the authority of the state.*

Among the passages from the Old Testament that Spinoza cites for the idea of the omnipotence of the Jewish state, there is, again, an utterly inconceivable example of his literary morality. He quotes the passage from the Sermon on the Mount that begins: "Love thy neighbor *and hate thine enemy.*"[252] He is so possessed by the idea of an equivalency between one who is alien by religion, one who is alien by citizenship, and, finally, one who is an enemy of the state that he not only ignores the numerous laws granting equal legal status to the *stranger*, but more than that: he does not know enough to call into question *the passage in the Sermon on the Mount on hating one's enemy, which is unknown in the entire Old Testament.*

By contrast, if, as the text-immanent[253] study of the Bible would require, he had directed his mind to the moral and poetic position of the stranger

in the Pentateuch and the Prophets, then of course his entire theory
would have been rendered baseless. But he also would have been spared

|359| the final conclusion that arises from his wisdom: "All these considerations
clearly show that religion has always been adapted to the good of the
commonwealth."[254] However, the laws concerning the stranger in ancient
Israel were a component of its monotheism, and the [laws of the] Noahide
represent a consistent extension of its religious politics.

Any final philosophical judgment of the *Theological-Political Treatise*
depends on one's judgment of the *Ethics*. We will not concern ourselves
with that relationship here. We have also endeavored as much as possible
to abstain from passing judgment on Spinoza's *personal character*. Nothing
is more delicate and difficult than passing judgment on the moral character
of an author, and even more so the character of a man who has had broad
cultural influence. It is not at all our place to judge the *man*, but only to
judge his philosophy and his scholarly oeuvre. Since his own day, the image
of his moral character—and actually of his intellectual character too—has
varied, in both the philosophical and the theological literature. Not until
recently did new problems come to light on account of new information on
Spinoza's engagement in the politics of his day.

However, when one presents and elucidates an author's religious and
political views, a moral judgment on the author is inevitable, and will
always be expressed between the lines. Everyone reads a work with his own
scholarly, religious, and political judgment, especially a work that examines
the Bible and weighs the validity of the two Testaments. The Christian is
permitted to remain a Christian; for the man of culture, nothing is superior
to Christianity, or to *the teaching of Christ*. All the philosophers of the
Christian world have, by their own example, acknowledged and borne
witness to this guiding principle of the history of culture. In the same
conscious frame of mind, Arabs philosophized for Islam, and Jews for the
Bible.

Spinoza is the first philosopher who, having no positive personal stake
in his inherited religion, felt moved to judge and condemn it. Moreover,
he does not reject Judaism because he rejects religion altogether. Instead,

|360| without accepting Christianity or professing faith in it, he grants the teaching
of Christ priority over Jewish monotheism. He grants pantheism priority
over monotheism, in the spirit of Christ. And in keeping with this idea,
he interprets the New Testament as universal religion, whereas, in the Old
Testament, universality is absent. In that case, however, the Old Testament

cannot be religion. From there it is only a small step, which Spinoza then takes in his Bible research, to the conclusion that Judaism is not a religion, but only a Jewish political theory.

Thus concludes the demolition of his inherited religion, the religion of his origins, and the religion from which he received his first religious knowledge and instruction and his first *ethical* impulses.

Spinoza's repudiation of Judaism ran counter to all *enlightenment and tolerance* and demolished the religious value of Judaism itself. But it was preceded, *long before his excommunication*, by *alienation*. Here we find the same ambivalence in Spinoza's practical attitude as we found in the theoretical. He did not seek the company of freethinkers, although there were such in the country. Instead, he became intimately acquainted with a religious sect that was more liberal in its views on questions concerning the Bible, but on matters of dogma represented a concertedly orthodox position in Christian doctrine. In its church structure, too, the sect was bound by its discipline.[255] "The most precious possession of the church is the right of excommunication."[256] That was the motto of the sect with which Spinoza kept intimate company before the Jews, who had so often suffered a bitter fate at the hands of informers in their own midst, took the step of excommunicating one of their own, one in whose lineage, intellect, and erudition they had placed their greatest hopes.

Spinoza's verdict on Judaism has not yet received a fair assessment in the literature. If a Christian were to condemn the teachings of Christ, he would dig his own moral grave. A characteristic, recent example of this phenomenon is the manner in which people have come to terms with *Nietzsche*. A well-known theologian interpreted him as follows: *Nietzsche* is searching for the *Superman*; therefore he is searching for Christ. In this way a veil is draped over the Antichrist, and the historical anomaly disappears. However, when Spinoza, with merciless severity, makes his own nation[257] the object of contempt—at the very time that *Rembrandt* lived on |361| the same street and immortalized the ideal type of the Jew—no voice rises in protest against this *humanly incomprehensible* betrayal. No voice rises in protest when he disfigures the *one unique* God, the worship of whom forced him to flee Portugal and the Inquisition with his father. There can be only one explanation and a very welcome one: finally a Jew of consequence has conceded his own stubbornness—as if there had not been apostates in every age, and as if Spinoza himself had not let his own ambivalence slip by, refraining from conversion. Moreover, his ambivalence is evident in his statement that he found Christian dogmas incomprehensible, comparing them with the act of squaring a circle.[258] Yet he gave Christ priority over Moses, over Moses and the prophets. That alone suffices, even though he always added his reservations, even though it was always clear as day that he conceived of Christ within the framework of the illusion of pantheism. Just the same, these qualifications matter little; the isolated fact speaks for itself, in all its obtuseness: Spinoza condemned the religion into which he was born; he made his own nation the object of contempt. He is a character who struggled to break away from Jewish obstinacy and elevate himself to the plane of freedom of spirit. But to what freedom? Could it be freedom from religion? That is not the general view. His liberation refers to the insufferable monotheism by which Judaism incessantly seeks to set itself apart from the most ideal notions of Christianity. This is the historical task that Judaism has always taken upon itself and always will.

One can thus understand that Spinoza became a standard-bearer within Protestant culture after *Kant, even* while opposing Kant's philosophical position. Moses Mendelssohn had good reason for worrying himself to death over the insinuation that his friend Lessing was an unwitting Spinozist.[259] An even deeper and profoundly harmful reason was the declaration by *Friedrich Heinrich Jacobi*, the most dangerous opponent of the Enlightenment and of critical philosophy, that philosophy is simply |362| synonymous with Spinozism.[260] *Kant*, opposing Jacobi, adopted from Spinoza the learned opinion that Judaism was only a political constitution and therefore not a religion at all. However, Kant always regarded Spinoza with unease, distrust, and annoyance, not just because of his own systematic superiority, but because of his philosophical integrity.[261]

Soon thereafter the Romantics came along, for whom religion would not remain confined to "reason alone."[262] Instead, they sought to affirm Christianity in its dogmatic foundations, this in spite of Protestantism and in spite of skeptical Idealism. For them, pantheism was a convenient tool, and they made ample use of it. Pantheism, however, was supposed to be construed not as the dissolution of Christianity, but only as its philosophical justification, like its first phase. *Schleiermacher* himself was carried to extremes in his gushing tribute to Spinoza, at least while he was writing *On Religion: Speeches to Its Cultured Despisers*, of which one can say that it has no connection to his dogmatics.[263]

Thus, from every perspective, it is understandable that Spinoza has been canonized in the modern era. Why, then, would anyone take an interest in the question of whether Spinoza did or did not do justice to the religion into which he was born? The situation is even more ominous with regard to the general scholarly and moral assessment of Spinoza. *David Friedrich Strauss* chose the sentence on Christ from Spinoza's letter as the motto for his *Life of Jesus.*[264]

Meanwhile, in biblical scholarship it has been generally acknowledged that Spinoza did not have the faintest clue about the actual founders of Judaism, the prophets. His accomplishment in Bible criticism is limited to the field of the philological examination of sources. However, the spirit of the thing did not register at all, if not to say that he deliberately rejected it. This issue is not a literary question; rather, it is clear from the present discussion that this book[265] came to be regarded as the confession of a crown witness who, by virtue of his philosophical genius and expertise in |363| the field of Judaism, possessed unassailable authority.

Thus, the book came to function as a leitmotif in literature at large, beyond the field of philosophy and its development. *Heine* recognized this fully, with his authentic Jewish anguish.[266] Even the world of *belles lettres* suffered from the charm of this pantheistic delusion, quite aside from the damage pantheism has inflicted on religious integrity by playing its ambiguous sport with God and man. That it is possible for anti-Semitism to celebrate its orgies in our age, at the same time as academic Protestant theology has produced illuminating studies that have led to a new understanding of Israelite prophecy—this would be inexplicable if not for the demonic spirit of Spinoza, still poisoning the atmosphere from within and without. The pithy sayings Spinoza employed to vent his vengeful hatred of the Jews can be found even now, almost verbatim, in the newspapers of those political camps.[267]

Now, I should like to say that the question may well arise for every reader, as for me, whether anyone else has formed a judgment on Spinoza as an author, with the same anger or indignation, however reserved. Thus, I should like, in conclusion, to cite the remarks of a man who has written a biography of Spinoza based on the most exacting examination of the sources, a man universally recognized as a scholar who is even-tempered in observation, in the collection of evidence, in judgment, in his attitudes, and in his scholarly and religious convictions altogether. Equally expert in Jewish sources and in the general sources of religion and philosophy, he has devoted his entire life to research on Spinoza. I am referring to *Freudenthal's* observations and conclusions on Spinoza.

If we wish to give a proper assessment of Freudenthal's characterization of Spinoza, we have to acknowledge that he has judged the religious issue from a position that is universal, not denominational. According to Freudenthal, in this treatise Spinoza did "no damage" to religion.[268] |364| Freudenthal also makes no distinction between the use of a biblical verse for pantheistic ends and the actual meaning of the verse. He goes so far as to say: "in no passage in the *Treatise* does [Spinoza] contest the biblical doctrine of God."[269] That statement conflicts, however, with Spinoza's view of the meaning of the one, unique God in the five books of Moses. Likewise, we cannot concur with the statement that Spinoza "was never carried away with making inappropriate or unfair assertions about divine revelation."[270] Furthermore, Freudenthal misunderstands the irony in the claim that prophecy derives from "supernatural knowledge,"[271] which, for Spinoza, is a fiction. The demonic aspect of Spinoza's character escapes Freudenthal altogether.

He emphasizes Spinoza's affinity, in his religious views, for the *Mennonites*, the *Collegiants*, and the *Socinians*. "Nevertheless, the gap between him and these sects cannot be bridged... What a distance remains between Spinoza's pantheistic philosophy and all such views! He mocks the extravagances of these fanatics."[272] Still, Freudenthal himself must concede: "The *Treatise* teaches us nothing different from the other works, but without the clarity and *candor* that we otherwise encounter in Spinoza."[273] On *Christology* he writes: Spinoza claimed "neither to want to discuss it, nor to deny it; but not to understand it. However, from his letters we learn that he declared it to be *absurd*."[274] Nevertheless, Freudenthal seeks to demonstrate Spinoza's sympathy and piety toward Christianity.

Still, Freudenthal does not mask the lack of clarity in Spinoza's general style: "The wording of this book, the *Theological-Political Treatise*, in which he gives his most thorough treatment of religion and theology, is often *obscure* and *misleading*. *Not infrequently* Spinoza appears to *affirm* what he *later retracts, not infrequently he appears to acknowledge* what he in other places *denies*. Occasionally we doubt whether he is speaking in his *own* name, or in the name of *another*. Often he employs well-known terms in a meaning that only he has given them... and he does not always indicate *distinctly* or *precisely* his own understanding of these terms."[275] From among the reasons Freudenthal cites for all of this, one should call attention to |365| the last: "The reason he is harsh in his criticism of the books of the *Old Testament*, but refrains from criticism of the *New*, is *allegedly* that he had no mastery of Greek."[276] Still, this need not have been a pretext, if only he had exercised circumspection and fairness in his comparative treatment of both Testaments.

Now Freudenthal also claims that *personal* motives are at work in Spinoza's character and temperament. "Along with other useful qualities, he inherited from his *forebears* a profound *need for peace*. They were not warriors hankering for battle, but hapless martyrs... thus they lost the capacity and courage for a fight that they had possessed in ancient times."[277] Here too I must object. The philosophers of the Middle Ages defended their esteemed Judaism with valiant candor against Islam and Christianity. Spinoza was the first to use *"care"* and *"caution, which occasionally went too far."*[278] Indeed, "Cautiously" (*caute*) was the motto on the seal of his ring. "One may call his caution *timidity."*[279] Nonetheless, in his attack on the reformed clergy he showed that "his valor was greater than his caution. Still, in Spinoza, there is *a mixture of courage and timidity, of valor and trepidation."*[280] Here Freudenthal gives Kant priority over Spinoza; but it is incorrect to state that "only fanatics of the truth... have the courage to speak the truth in all circumstances."[281] It is incorrect to state that in those times the most free of minds were coerced into "suppressing and denying the truth."[282] One need only think of *Jean Bodin*, who, in his *Heptaplomeres*, mounted the strongest sort of attacks on Christianity, while devoting the grandest glorification to Judaism.[283] It must seem conspicuous and odd that this book, which was known to Leibniz and Thomasius and which at the time circulated widely, should have remained unknown to Spinoza.

After considering a number of concrete issues, Freudenthal continues: "First of all, *one misjudges his character completely, if one attributes to him mainly tenderness and gentleness of feeling."*[284] Here is where Freudenthal's portrait of Spinoza's character begins in earnest: "Spinoza is good by nature... but he is no man of feeling... so great is the power of his intellect |366| that occasionally a certain *sobriety and aloofness* surface in his nature."[285] Freudenthal sees a connection between this and Spinoza's aesthetic obtuseness. And yet Spinoza did not succeed in "subjecting his emotional life entirely to the control of the intellect. By birth, he was not free from *violent emotional swings*... He reported to us himself [...] that in his youth he had allowed himself to be dazzled by the brilliance of wealth, honor, and lust... but he never himself realized the ideal of the detached Stoic wise man."[286]

On occasion, pain and anger, aversion and fear, *disturb his equanimity...* Under the cloak of a sober intellect [...] there still burns a fire, even at this time [i.e., in his adulthood], which occasionally erupts with violent force... He turns on the pettiness of the rabbis, the fantasies of the kabbalist, and the subtleties of the Scholastics with a *vehemence* that is doubly conspicuous in the Spinoza who is otherwise so lenient in his judgments. "The rabbis are insane, the Bible exegetes are dreamers, invent falsehood..., the Scholastics seem after a fashion to strive for error and to contrive the most absurd things." These are some of the pithy expressions of anger with which Spinoza airs his views on errant trends in theology and philosophy.

He often reserves similar language for his personal opponents... Did this man, who was so rich in love, also allow space for *hatred*? One could be tempted to assume so when one considers the *repulsive severity* with which he passes judgment not only on his opponents, but also on the *great multitudes of the nation* among whom he lived, and on the *nation of his origin.*[287]

He believed that *the masses*

regard piety, fear of God, and fortitude simply as burdens that one casts off after death and for which one receives a reward... He pays no heed to the fact that the nation he criticizes so severely was valiant, industrious, patriotic, strong-willed, and firm in its faith... With the same trenchancy he passes judgment on the characteristics, history, and Scriptures of the Jewish nation. *He exposes its shortcomings and errors with merciless cruelty. He has no eye for its virtues.* He who has so much to criticize in the Old Testament *finds not a word for the sublimity of prophetic discourse, for the intellectual richness of Job, for the inward piety of the Psalms.* He must have been in thrall to a *loathing* that *blinded* him to the good sides of his ethnic compatriots[288] when, for purposes of *disparaging* his own nation, he bases himself on the *slanders of the Samaritans* and the animosities of *Tacitus*, who was ill informed on Jewish life. He must have been in thrall to the same loathing when he, the great expert on the Bible, imputes the *commandment to hate one's enemy* to the Old Testament, because it is *falsely* attributed to it in the Gospel of Matthew. Finally, the same loathing must account for the fact that he could find no explanation for the *miraculous survival* of the Jewish nation other than the hatred of other nations and the sign of circumcision.[289]

|367|

According to Freudenthal, he was "guided by anxiety, caution, and a fear of men."[290] "And despite the courage he often demonstrated, he was apparently subject to unmanly fears. That is, in any case, the opinion for which we argue here.[291] *It is prejudice if one regards him as a saint.*"[292] To be sure, Freudenthal then makes an effort to defend him, saying: "There are no saints on earth."[293] But it does matter in what way someone has demonstrated that he is not a saint. What is especially disturbing in the unfairness of Spinoza's literary judgment is "the *fear* that gives the *Theological-Political Treatise* its particular tone."[294] It was fear that drove him to apply a double standard to the Old and New Testaments.

Two factors weigh against Spinoza: his contempt for the common *people* and his repugnant hatred for the *Jews*. "He judges the common folk of Holland with narrow-minded harshness."[295] Certainly neither *Jan Steen's* nor *Ostade's* paintings can corroborate his view.[296] "He criticizes the Jewish people with the same bitter narrow-mindedness... One should not, however, use the wrong name for the emotion that produced all of his harsh and, in part, unjust observations. One should not label as *hatred* someone's disdain for his opponents, or for the members of his people or nation.[297] His |368| aversion bore no trace of a desire to inflict harm, without which real hatred is unthinkable."[298]

Here I cannot entirely agree with Freudenthal. First of all, it may well be possible to conceive of hatred without the desire to do harm. Furthermore, such a desire cannot be ruled out in a man of high intelligence, unless he is also attentive to the *risk* of such harm and takes precautions against it. In addition, even if Spinoza reviewed his own words in the most superficial way, he can have had no doubt that the judgments he had drawn from Scripture and [Jewish] worship could do great and immediate harm to the Jews. To rule out hatred, it is not sufficient merely to deny intent to do harm. In the case of Judaism and the Jews, the mere lack of caution suffices as proof of hatred, particularly when such a lack of caution presents itself in such an astounding form. One should also note what Freudenthal says elsewhere: "Moreover, *it is conspicuous how careful* he was to spare the *New* Testament in his criticism. He also did not directly attack Christian dogmas."[299] And still more: "Spinoza... *deliberately shrouded* what he teaches about revelation and prophecy *in semi-obscurity*."[300] On the basis of this careful assessment, one may well say this much at least: that Spinoza, in his attitude toward Jews and Judaism, was of an unnatural frame of mind and disposition.

I could just as well say, of disposition and mind, placing the emphasis on the latter. For it is certain that one can arrive at a proper assessment of a great thinker only when one brackets all secondary circumstances and finds the sought-after explanation in the foundations of his *mind*. This appears to be the case for Spinoza as well.

The great scholar of the Bible *never attained an understanding of prophecy*. This is why it was so easy for him, taking pantheism as his point of departure, to be steered into Christology; for he never understood prophetic messianism and its [idea of] the future of humanity. It does not bode well for the formalism of pantheism if it contents itself with |369| equating God and nature, and then instantly makes man into God. It is unperturbed by the question of what then becomes of the human beings and nations on earth. In this kind of pantheism a future for humanity is impossible, because the "common people" can never mature into a condition of internalized morality, can never grow sufficiently to acquire genuine knowledge.[301]

This *difference*, too, between *religion and philosophy* is part and parcel of the intellectual structure of *a pantheism that purports to advance enlightenment*. [The ideal of] universal humanity requires the removal of the barrier between the knowledge of philosophers and the religion of the common people, as ancient messianism expressed this requirement in its own language. Spinoza, however, maintains his aristocratic prejudice. In keeping with the historical purpose of this political tract, he deviates from this prejudice only superficially, and defends it vigorously and without a murmur of a doubt in the *Political Treatise*.

The intellectual motives do not end there. It is a typical sign of the *Enlightenment*, as it was constituted *before the German* Enlightenment (even if the former anticipated the latter), that an *antagonism* persisted *between knowledge and culture on the one hand and religion on the other*. Thus, the antagonism also persisted, sometimes more severely, sometimes less so, between *higher and lower classes of people*. It would be worthwhile to investigate whether such an idea occurs in Herder, in Lessing, or in Moses Mendelssohn. In *Kant*, it would be an impossibility. However, if *religious Enlightenment* is not infused with authentic and sincere convictions about *social universalism*, then freethinking remains nothing but a revolt against religion. Religion will not be shaken by such a tempest in a teapot. Religion can be promoted only by means of its own vital strengths, which it can draw only from within, and which become effective only when both science and philosophy enter into this same source, bringing it to life and making it fruitful *for all human beings without exception.*

In this context we must think of *Fichte* in particular, for he discerned the deepest national forces at work in the lower classes and called on these forces specifically to serve the cause of the universal regeneration of nation and humanity.[302] *Our German Enlightenment had already accomplished the transition to scientific Idealism*[303] *in Kant.* Kant's political writing marks the great divide between the Enlightenment and scientific philosophy, with regard to both religion and politics. From this vantage point it is also thoroughly understandable that Kant felt repulsed by Spinoza. |370|

There is also no need whatsoever to presume an unusual knowledge of psychology in order to fathom Spinoza's psyche. It suffices to reduce his frame of mind to one clear formulation: he lacks any inner disposition toward scientific Idealism. He shows no sign that he understands Plato. What he learned and appropriated from Descartes concerns only the Scholastic weakness that connects Descartes, a truly great thinker, to the waning of his century. However, Descartes himself was one of the first to usher in the age of the "new sciences." Spinoza is not a Cartesian in the spirit of Descartes, in the sense of a new idealist who proceeds from the certainty of knowledge to nature, which is based on it. Spinoza is a Scholastic equipped with new terms: *nature, necessity,* and *natural law.* And he is a Scholastic in the best sense, to the extent that he takes the *ontological concept of God* as his point of departure and does not advance beyond it.

He demonstrates his indebtedness to Scholastic thought not only in the formalism of his terminological system, but more vividly in his *indifference to the modern question of law and the state.* His *English following* is telling, just as with the question of law, in contrast to *Bacon,* and in this case to *Hobbes.* Whatever differences may be discernible, his position, in principle, is that right derives from might, just as laws are derived from induction. He has no admiration for the English *Revolution:* he holds that, in the end, everything remained unchanged anyway. He does not have an eye for the creative *national forces* that stir in the depths of the life of a state. At this point I believe one can finally say the reason is this: *his heart was inclined neither to conjure up nor to discern* these eternal, deep, and truly creative forces.

Spinoza represents a grave impediment to modern Jewish history, and therefore a great misfortune. Until Lessing and Herder, Christians of all stripes had spurned Spinoza—not just the dogmatic fanatics, but no less |371|

than Leibniz and Thomasius. However, ever since Lessing and Herder placed Spinoza on a pedestal, he and his *Tractatus* have become the authentic source of biblical and rabbinic Judaism in the modern world.[304] Moses Mendelssohn innocently contributed to this erroneous assessment of Judaism. But he also compensated for his unintended affirmation of Spinoza through all the good that he achieved for the correct understanding of Judaism, by virtue of his erudition and his profound and genuine enlightenment. Thus Spinoza remains the real accuser of Judaism in the eyes of the Christian world.

Nonetheless, I should like to say: this great enemy who emerged from our midst is *our best witness, against his own will*. No one who holds the views that constitute Spinoza's intellectual framework will acquire a love or understanding of Judaism. Now it is understandable that mystics are not satisfied by the transcendence of the one, unique God. However, history has taught us that pantheism in itself does not stand in contradiction to monotheism. Mendelssohn rightly raised that point long ago, in his argument against Jacobi. But what is absolutely incompatible with a vital, personal Judaism is the *complete absence of prophetic religion, the complete absence of an inward relationship to the idea of a messianic future of humanity* and to its *roots*, which lie in *the social legislation promulgated by Moses*. Whoever takes these laws, like the *Sabbath*, simply as ceremonies, and not as the "true way of life," is using this example to establish a distinction between Bible criticism and philosophy of religion. Spinoza notes that the law of the Sabbath undergoes a change when the Decalogue is repeated; but he has no appreciation of the importance of showing *what* the change is. His

|372| confused relationship to prophetic religion explains his similar relationship to inwardness, to poetry, to the religion of the *Psalms*. If the Psalms do not touch one's heart, then one cannot understand Jewish *prayer*. And without the compass of Jewish prayer, one is unable to understand anything of the history of the Jews.

This fundamental flaw in Spinoza's ethical and religious nature explains not only his errors in judgment and the truculence with which he states them. It also explains why the entire composition comprises such heterogeneous elements as we have encountered in the discrete goals of this treatise.

Just as he bases the *state* on *aristocracy*, and *religion* on a *natural faith that is irrevocably void of philosophical understanding*, so was he able to set about examining not just the *composition* of the Old Testament. He took on the further task—making it his *main task*—to illuminate and assess Old Testament *teachings* concerning *religion* and *state*, *Israel* and the *nations*, *justice* and blessedness, in the context of a book that deals with the theoretical questions of state and religion. Whoever is able to form an understanding of the prophets solely in the light of Christ certainly cannot have understood Moses in his own right. And if one has not understood Moses and the prophets in their uniqueness, the later history of Judaism will remain an enigma, rendered comprehensible only by the hatred of the nations, their response to the hatred that Jews, as required by their religion(!), direct at them.

Spinoza suppressed the concept of the *Noahide*: as a term in constitutional law it represents an astonishing manifestation of the universal idea of natural religion, in the form of the fundamental idea of Jewish monotheism.

NOTES

1. Cohen is referring to Jakob Freudenthal, ed., *Die Lebensgeschichte Spinozas in Quellenschriften, Urkunden und nichtamtlichen Nachrichten* (Leipzig: Veit & Comp., 1889). For a more recent biography of Spinoza, see Steven M. Nadler, *Spinoza: A Life* (Cambridge and New York: Cambridge University Press, 1999). For Cohen's assessment of Freudenthal, see pp. 51ff. [RSS]

2. Johan de Witt (1625-1672) was councilor pensionary, the political leader of Holland, from 1653 until 1672. His assassination at the hands of a rioting mob shook Spinoza deeply. [RSS]

3. The title of the Dutch political leader; see previous note. [RSS]

4. Carl Gebhardt, *Baruch de Spinoza, Theologisch-politischer Traktat*, vol. 93 of *Philosophische Bibliothek*, 3rd ed. (Leipzig: Dürr'sche Buchhandlung, 1908), "Einleitung," pp. viii (first quotation), ix (second quotation).

5. Jean Maximilien Lucas is purportedly the author of the first Spinoza biography, published in 1719 under the title *La vie de Spinosa*. See A. Wolf, ed., *The Oldest Biography of Spinoza*, with translation, introduction, annotations, etc. (Port Washington, N.Y.: Kennikat Press, 1927; reprint, 1970). [RSS]

6. Gebhardt, "Einleitung," p. ix.

7. The terms "philology" and "philological" have had a broad range in German, encompassing not just linguistic analysis, but also textual analysis, historical reconstruction, and interpretation, a semantic field that the English term "philology" used to cover, lost, and has recovered in recent years. [RSS]

8. Gebhardt, "Einleitung," p. vif.

9. Matthew 7:1. [RSS]

10. Ferdinand Tönnies, *Thomas Hobbes der Mann und der Denker*, 2nd expanded ed. (Stuttgart: Fr. Frommann, n.d.), p. 230 n. 48.

11. This foundation, however, is no longer purely philological. If one were to call it theological, one would still have to search for a reason. That reason lies indisputably in Spinoza's philosophy, in which his concepts of state and religion are both ultimately grounded.

12. Gebhardt, "Einleitung," p. xi; for the next quotation, p. xif.

13. Carl Siegfried, *Spinoza als Kritiker und Ausleger des Alten Testaments: Ein Beitrag zur Geschichte des alttestamentlichen Kritik und Exegese* (*Nebst dem Jahresbericht des Rectors [...] der Königlichen Landesschule Pforta*) (Naumburg: H. Sieling, 1867). "After this sampling, we cannot regret that the philosopher did not engage further in biblical exegesis [...] very strange things would certainly have emerged" (p. 50). After considering matters such as Spinoza's aesthetic judgment on the "nugae" of poetry, through the example of *Orlando furioso*, about which he had apparently heard, Siegfried states: "No wonder that, in [Spinoza's] hands, life and soul harden into stone" (p. 51 n. 2). Finally, he writes: "Who could not, just like Spinoza, take the stage as a self-appointed exegete of Holy Scripture, *since [Spinoza] lacks any understanding of the ethical motives at work in true religiosity[?]... He has not even understood the fundamentals of prophetic religion*" (p. 52). Siegfried also defends Maimonides against Spinoza (p. 53).

14. *Quid autem Deus sit et qua ratione res omnes videat... haec et similia Scriptura ex professo, et tanquam aeternam veritatem [i.o. doctrinam] non docet.* One should note here, as everywhere, Spinoza's qualified manner of expression. He does not state directly that Scripture simply does not teach this. *Tractatus theologico-politicus*, in *Benedicti de Spinoza Opera, quotquot reperta sunt*, ed. J. van Vloten and J.P.N. Land, 2nd ed. (The Hague: Martin Nijhoff, 1895), vol. 1, chs. 1-3, pp. 347-396, chs. 4-20 in vol. 2, pp. 1-173. For this passage: Gebhardt, vol. 3, pp. 102-103; CW 460.

15. *His accedit quod Scriptura nullam Dei definitionem expresse tradit... ex quibus omnibus concludimus, intellectualem Dei cognitionem... ad fidem et religionem revelata nullo modo pertineret et [...] homines circa hanc sine scelere toto coelo errare posse.* (Gebhardt 3:171; CW 513).

16. *Nihil cum philosophia commune habere.* (Gebhardt 3:10)

17. *Sed cum in iis, quae scriptura expresse docet, nihil reperissem, quod cum intellectu non conveniret, nec quod eidem repugnaret.* (Gebhardt 3:10)

18. "Faculty of knowledge" is a rendering of the German *Erkenntnis*, which can indicate either the capacity for cognition, hence "faculty of knowledge," or the result of cognition, "knowledge" itself. The reader should be aware that "faculty of knowledge," "knowledge," and occasionally "cognition" all lead back to the same German word. [RSS]

19. Spinoza's "negation," to which Cohen refers here, is the denial of any connection between reason and faith. [RSS]

20. *Intentum Scripturae esse tantum, obedientiam docere. [...] Quis enim non videt utrumque Testamentum nihil esse praeter obedientiae disciplinam.* (Gebhardt 3:174; CW 515)

21. Here, as elsewhere, the term "science" is a translation of the German *Wissenschaft*. Unlike the English term "science," which encompasses only the

natural and social sciences, *Wissenschaft* includes humanistic inquiry as well. For Cohen, *Wissenschaft* implies a system. [RSS]

22. *Ethica*, bk. 2, prop. 49, coroll. [HW] (CW 273) ["Intellect and will are one and the same."—RSS]

23. Cohen translates in the plural ("concepts") where both Gebhardt's German and the original Latin have a singular: *conceptus simplex mentis divinae* ("the simple concept of the divine mind"). The English translation here follows Shirley, CW 392. [RSS]

24. *Verbum Dei revelatum non esse... sed conceptum simplicem mentis divinae prophetis revelatae; scilicet Deo integro animo obedire, justitiam et charitatem colendo.* (Gebhardt 3:10; CW 392)

25. CW 392.

26. James 2:17. [HW]

27. *Sequitur deinde [i.o.] denique fidem non tam requirere vera quam pia dogmata, hoc est talia, quae animum ad obedientiam movent, tametsi inter ea plurima sint, quae nec umbram veritatis habent; dummodo tamen is, qui eadem amplectitur, eadem falsa esse ignoret. [...] Cum itaque uniuscujisque fides... non ratione veritatis aut falsitatis pie vel impia sit habenda... hinc sequitur, ad fidem Catholicam sive universalem nulla dogmata pertinere, de quibus inter honestos potest dari controversia.* (Gebhardt 3:176-177; CW 516-517)

28. *Quandoquidem ex solis operibus sunt judicanda.* (Gebhardt 3:176-177; CW 517)

29. This particular quotation could not be found. Cf. Spinoza's "Preface" to the *Theological-Political Treatise* (Gebhardt 3:10: *Fundamentalibus deinde fidei ostensis, concludo denique, objectum cognitionis revelatae nihil esse praeter obedientiam.* CW 392). See also chs. 13 and 14. [HW]

30. *Deum, hoc est ens supremum* (But here begins the definition of God's essence!) *[...] existere, qui enim nescit, vel non credit, ipsum existere, ei obedire nequit.* (Gebhardt 3:177)

31. *Eum esse unicum.* (Gebhardt 3:177; CW 517.) [In the translation by Gebhardt that Cohen used alongside the original Latin, *unicum* ("one alone") is rendered as *einzig*. The meaning "unique" for *einzig* is the foundational concept of Cohen's philosophy of religion: "The Uniqueness of God" ("Die Einzigkeit Gottes"), topic of the first chapter of Cohen's *Religion of Reason out of the Sources of Judaism*, indicates that the meaning of monotheism lies in the idea of a unique ontological category, not merely in the reduction to one in number. Hence, throughout this translation, I have rendered *einzig*, when used in relation to God, as "one and unique."—RSS]

32. Cohen uses the German *Erkenntnis* ("knowledge" or "cognition") here,

and *Wissen* ("knowledge") in the previous paragraph. Where *Erkenntnis* refers more to the function than to the content of knowledge, I translate "cognition." [RSS]

33.   *Caeterum, quid Deus, sive illud verae vitae exemplar sit: an scilicet sit ignis, spiritus lux, cogitation, etc., id nihil ad fidem; ... Haec, et similia, inquam, nihil refert, in respectu fidei, qua ratione unusquisque intelligat.* (Gebhardt 3:178; CW 518.)

34.   *Ostendimus enim, fidem non tam veritatem, quam pietatem exigere.* (Gebhardt 3:179; CW 518)

35.   *Quae doctrina quam salutaris quamque necessaria sit in republica.* (Gebhardt 3:179; CW 519)

36.   *Deinde Philosophiae fundamenta notiones communes sunt... Fidei autem (sc. fundamenta)* [Cohen's emendation is enclosed in parentheses]: *historiae, et lingua, et ex sola Scriptura, et revelatione petenda* [not out of nature or reason!]. (Gebhardt 3:179; CW 519)

37.   *Absolute igitur concludimus, quod nec Scriptura rationi, nec ratio Scripturae accomodanda sit.* (Gebhardt, 3:185; CW 523-524)

38.   See below, p. 42. [HW]

39.   By "that problematic historical fact," Cohen seems to mean the Stoic idea he paraphrases in the previous paragraph: that nature is both the logical and the historical origin of all culture. [RSS]

40.   German: *Nebenbegriff.* [RSS]

41.   The allusion in this paragraph is obscure. Cohen may have in mind the view of the celebrated Stoic philosopher Posidonius of Apamea (c. 135–c. 51-50 BCE), who calls attention to climate as one factor affecting the body, which, in turn, dictates the "movements of the soul." But the allusion is too fragmentary to track down with any certainty. (See F. Jacoby, *Die Fragmente der griechischen Historiker* [Leiden: E.J. Brill, 1961], vol. IIa, p. 282, frag. 102) [RSS]

42.   *Prius de Jure Naturali uniuscuiusque, ad Rempublicam et Religionem nondum attendentes.* (Gebhardt 3:189; CW 526)

43.   *Per jus et institutum naturae nihil aliud intelligo, quam regulas naturae uniuscuiusque individui.* (Gebhardt 3:189; CW 526)

44.   *Ex. gr. pisces a natura determinati sunt ad natandum, magni ad minores comedendum, adeoque pisces summo naturali iure aqua potiuntur, et magni minores comedunt. Nam certum est, naturam absolute consideratam jus cummum habere ad omnia, quae potest, hoc est, jus naturae eo usque se extendere, quo usque ejus potentia se extendit; naturae enim potentia ipsa Dei potentia est, qui summum jus ad omnia habet.* (Gebhardt 3:189)

45.   *Quia universalis potentia totius naturae nihil est praeter potentiam omnium individuorum simul, hinc sequitur unumquodque individuum jus summum habere*

ad omnia, quae potest, sive ius uniuscujusque eo usque se extendere, quo usque ejus determinata potentia se extendit. (Gebhardt 3:189; CW 527)

46.   *Nec hic ullam cognoscimus [i.o. agnoscimus] differentiam inter homines et reliqua naturae individua.* (Gebhardt 3:189; CW 527)

47.   *Atque hoc idem est, quod Paulus docet, qui ante legem, hoc est, quamdiu homines ex naturae imperio vivere considerantur, nullum peccatum agnoscit.* (Gebhardt 3:190; CW 527)

48.   *Non enim omnes naturaliter determinati sunt ad operandum secundum regulas et leges rationis.* (Gebhardt 3:190; CW 527)

49.   Cohen's original reads: "*Recht und Gesetz,*" which is construed here as a hendiadys. [RSS]

50.   *Jus et Institutum naturae... non contentiones, non odia, non iram, non dolos...* (Gebhardt 3:190; CW 528)

51.   *Nam natura non legibus humanae rationis [...] intercluditur.* (Gebhardt 3:190-191; CW 528)

52.   *Quidquid [i.o. Quicquid] ergo nobis in natura ridiculum, absurdum, aut malum videtur.* (Gebhardt 3:191; CW 528f)

53.   *Ex quibus concludimus pactum nullam vim habere posse, nisi ratione utilitatis, qua sublata pactum simul tollitur, et irritum manet.* (Gebhardt 3:192; CW 529)

54.   *Democratia vocatur, quae proinde definitur cultus [i.o. coetus] universus hominum, qui collegialiter summum ius ad omnia, quae potest, habet.* (Gebhardt 3:193; CW 530)

55.   *De quo prae omnibus agere malui, quia maxime naturale videbatur, et maxime ad libertatem, quam natura unicuique concedit, accedere.* (GEbhardt 3:195; CW 531)

56.   [*Tractatus Politicus: ...sed simul vidimus, viam, quam ipsa Ratio docet, perarduam esse; ita ut,] qui sibi persuadent posse multitudinem, vel qui sibi publicis negotiis distrahuntur, induci, ut ex solo Rationis praescripto vivant, seculum Poëtarum aureum, seu fabulam somnient.* (Gebhardt 3:275; CW 682)

57.   In *Political Treatise*, 10.9 (CW 751), Spinoza states: "So since we have shown that the fundamental laws of both kinds of aristocracy are in conformity with reason and with the common sentiments of men, we can therefore affirm that, if any states can be everlasting, these will necessarily be so; that is to say, they cannot be destroyed by any avoidable cause, but only by some unavoidable fatality." [HW/RSS]

58.   *Transeo tandem ad tertium, et omnino absolutum imperium, quod Democraticum appelamus.* (Gebhardt 3:358; CW 752)

59.   Gebhardt, "Einleitung," p. xx. [In reference to Ludwig (Lodewijk) Meyer, *Philosophia S. Scripturae Interpres* (Eleutheropolis [Amsterdam], 1666).—HW]

60.   *Nam is et natura et tempore prior est religione.* (Gebhardt 3:198; CW 533)

61.   *Quare ante revelationem nemo jure divino, quod non potest non ignorare, tenetur. [...] Quare absolute concedendum ius divinum ab eo tempora incepisse, a quo homines expresso pacto Deo promiserunt in omnibus obedire, quo sua libertate naturali quasi concesserunt [i.o. cesserunt], jusque suum in Deum transtulerunt sicuti in statu civili fieri diximus.* (Gebhardt 3:198; CW 534)

62.   *Quod si summa potestas nollet Deo in jure suo revelato obedire, id ipsi cum suo periculo, et damno licet [nullo scilicet jure civili vel naturali repugnante].* (Gebhardt 3:199; CW 534)

63.   *Et Deum nullum singulare regnum in homines habere, nisi per eos, qui imperium tenent.* (Gebhardt 3:295; CW 558)

64.   *At quod cultus justitiae et charitatis vim juris non posse accipere, nisi ex jure imperii.* [This quotation is a combination of two similar sentences that occur close to one another. The translated quotation in the text, however, refers to a third passage: *(Justitia et) proximum charitatis, a solo imperii jure (...) vim juris et mandati accipiunt*—HW] (Gebhardt 3:295-296; CW 559)

65.   CW 559.

66.   This particular remark about the state could not be identified. By the context, it fits chapter 19, which, toward the end, treats the right of the state to intervene in matters of religion. In the Christian state, unlike in the state of the Hebrews, such intervention was never possible without "grave danger of sedition and harm to religion" (CW 564). (Gebhardt 3:237: *numquam nisi magno seditionum pericula, et religionis detrimento*). [HW]

67.   *Notatu dignum est, quod Prophetae, viri scilicet privati, libertate sua monendi, increpandi, et exprobrandi homines magis irritaverunt quam correxerunt; qui tamen a Regibus moniti vel castigati facile flectebantur, Imo Regibus etiam piis saepe intolerabiles fuerunt.* (Gebhardt 3:223; CW 553f.)

68.   CW 553f.

69.   CW 394.

70.   Ibid.

71.   *Certa cognitio a Deo hominibus revelata.* (Gebhardt 3:15; CW 394)

72.   *Cognitionem naturalem Prophetiam vocari posse.* (Gebhardt 3:15; CW 394)

73.   Cf., for example, René Descartes, *Méditations* III, ed. Adam/Tannery, IX, p. 30: *Je ne saurais rien révoquer en doute de ce que la lumière naturelle me fait voir*

être vrais, ainsi qu'elle m'a tantôt fait voir que, de ce que je doutas, je pouvais conclure que j'étais (cited according to *Œuvres philosophiques*, II, p.436). [HW]

74. Cf. *Méditations* VI, ed. Adam/Tannery, IX p. 64: *Par la nature, considérée en général, je n'entends maintenant autre chose que Dieu même, ou bien l'ordre et la disposition que Dieu a établie dans les choses créés* (cited according to *Œuvres philosophiques*, II, p. 491). [HW]

75. See Cohen's interpretation of Descartes in *Kants Theorie der Erfahrung*, 2nd ed. (Berlin: Ferdinand Dümmler, 1885), pp. 26-42; on "general rules" in relation to Descartes' "Regulae ad directionem ingenii," see also p. 30f. [HW]

76. *Nam ea, quae lumine naturali cognoscimus, a sola Dei cognitione, ejusque aeternis decretis dependent.* (Gebhardt 3:15; CW 394)

77. נביא. *Propheta enim apud Hebreos vocatur nabi [id est orator et interpres].* (Gebhardt 3:15) [Cohen truncated the sentence in his citation; his claim is supported by the continuation, which he did not cite.—RSS]

78. *Quandoquidem Dei natura, quatenus de ea participamus, Deique decreta eam nobis quasi dictant.* (Gebhardt 3:15; CW 395)

79. *Quod Judaei nunquam causarum mediarum, sive particularium faciunt mentionem, ... sed... ad Deum semper recurrunt.* (Gebhardt 3:16; CW 395)

80. *Quod omnia... iis revelata fuerunt vel verbis, vel figuris, vel utroque hoc modo.* (Gebhardt 3:17; CW 396)

81. German: *Vorstellung*. In colloquial German, *Vorstellung* means "idea" or "thought," but in the Kantian terminology employed by Cohen, it refers to any content of consciousness and is usually translated "representation." [RSS]

82. *Voce enim vera revelavit Deus Mosi leges.* (Gebhardt 3:17; CW 396)

83. Gebhardt 3:17: "ונועדתי לך שם ודברתי אתך מעל הכפרת מבין שני הכרובים" *et paratus ero tibi, et loquar tecum ex illa parte tegminis, quae est inter duos Cherubines."* (CW 396)

84. CW 396.

85. Ibid.

86. Ibid.

87. בלא אמצעי. In Ibn Ezra's commentary on the Pentateuch ad loc. [HW]

88. *Ut duo homines suos conceptus invicem, mediantibus suis duobus corporibus, communicare solent.* (Gebhardt 3:18; CW 396)

89. *Nec Lex, Mosi revelata... ut credamus, Deum esse in corporeum, nec etiam eum nullam habere imaginem, sive figuram, sed tantum Deum esse.* (Gebhardt 3:19; CW 397)

90.   *Quinimo Scriptura clare indicat Deum habere figuram, et Mosi, ubi Deum loquentem audiebat, eam aspexissse, nec tamen videre contigisse, nisi Dei posteriora.* (Gebhardt 3:19; CW 397)

91.   Deuteronomy 34:10; Gebhardt 3:20; CW 398. [HW]

92.   The full passage Cohen is citing is the following: "'And there stood [meaning 'arose'] not a prophet since in Israel like unto Moses, whom the Lord knew face to face,' which must be taken to mean 'through voice alone,' for not even Moses ever saw the Lord's face." (CW 398) [RSS]

93.   *Nam enim nullis mediis corporeis adhibitis, menti nostrae suam essentiam communicat.* (Gebhardt 3:20; CW 398)

94.   CW 398.

95.   In the *Complete Works*, Shirley usually translates *mens* as "mind," but here renders *sola mente* as "by pure intuition." I have retained "mind" for the sake of terminological consistency. [RSS]

96.   *Attamen ut homo aliquis sola mente aliqua perciperet, quae in primis nostrae cognitionis fundamentis non continentur..., ejus mens praestantior necessario, atque humana longe excellentior esse deberet.* (Gebhardt 3:20-21; CW 398) [Translation lightly edited.—RSS]

97.   *Quare non credo ullum alium ad tantam perfectionem supra alios pervenisse, praeter Christum, cui Dei placita [quae homines ad salutem ducunt] sine verbis, aut visionibus, sed immediate revelata sunt.* (Gebhardt 3:20-21; CW 398)

98.   *Et hoc sensu etiam dicere possumus, Sapientiam Dei, hoc est, Sapientiam, quae supra humanam est, naturam humanam in Christo assumpsisse, et Christum viam salutis fuisse.* (Gebhardt 3:20-21; CW 398)

99.   *Verum monere hic necesse est, me de iis, quae quaedam Ecclesiae de Christo statuunt, prorsus non loqui, neque ea negare; nam libenter fateor me ea non capere.* (Gebhardt 3:20-21; CW 398)

100.   Rijnsburg, not far from Leiden, had become the center of the radically anti-clerical and anti-dogmatic sect of the Collegiants, who held that the only true faith consisted not in adherence to dogma, but in obedience to God as understood from the unmediated study of Scripture. They were the target of a 1653 law "forbidding anti-trinitarian... 'conventicles' from meeting." On this and Spinoza's relations with the Collegiants in general, see Nadler, *Spinoza*, pp. 139-141. [RSS]

101.   CW 398.

102.   Letter 73 (to Henry Oldenburg. On Oldenburg, see below, n. 198.):

Finally, to disclose my meaning more clearly on the third head [Latin: *caput*, also "part" or "main point"—RSS], I say that for salvation it is not altogether necessary to know Christ according to the flesh; but with regard to the *eternal* son of God, *that is, God's eternal wisdom,* which has manifested itself in all things and chiefly in the human mind, and most of all in Christ Jesus, a very different view must be taken. For without this no one can attain to a state of blessedness, since this alone teaches what is true and false, good and evil. And since, as I have said, this wisdom has been manifested most of all through Jesus Christ... As to the additional teaching of certain churches, that God took upon himself human nature, I have expressly indicated that I do not understand what they say. Indeed, to tell the truth, they seem to me to speak no less *absurdly* than one who might tell me that a circle has taken on the nature of a square. (CW 943).

These remarks about Jesus were used by David Friedrich Strauss as the motto for his *Leben Jesu,* about Jesus as the eternal son of God and as God's eternal wisdom. On the other hand, they also refer to Christ Jesus, in whom that divine wisdom, which is contained in *all* things, but most of all in the human mind, is most revealed. These remarks contain all the ambiguity of this disingenuous kind of pantheism and of the Bible criticism it inspired. [Strauss (1808-1874) argued in his *Das Leben Jesu, kritisch bearbeitet* (German original, 1835-1836); English translation: *The Life of Jesus, Critically Examined* (London: SCM Press, 1973) that the Gospels are myth, and that it is absurd to attribute divine attributes to an individual, though the divine may have become incarnate in humankind as a whole. Cf. Van A. Harvey, "Strauss, David Friedrich," *Encyclopedia of Religion,* ed. Lindsay Jones, 2nd ed., vol. 13 (Detroit: Macmillan Reference USA, 2005), pp. 8747-8748.—RSS] [Cf. p. 80 and note 264.] It is also interesting that Spinoza makes *blessedness* dependent on such wisdom. He thus assumes a stance that is prior to the Noahides (cf. p. 58). Nevertheless, his correspondent was not satisfied by this concession. He demands belief in resurrection as well. (letter 79; CW 953-954) Spinoza will concede resurrection only in an allegorical sense. However, he assumes the life, passion, death, and burial are literal accounts. (letter 78; CW 952-953)

103.   *Quod quidam Hebraeorum quasi per nebulam vidisse videntur, qui scilicet statuunt, Deum, Dei intellectum resque ab ipso intellectas unum et idem esse.* (*Ethica,* bk. 2, prop. 7,. schol. [Gebhardt 2:90; CW 247]) This equation has been stated by many, in particular by Maimonides: שכל = משכיל = מושכל. (Cf. *Guide of the Perplexed,* vol. 1, p. 68, in the first sentence: "He is the intellect as well as the intellectually cognizing subject and the intellectually cognized object" [Moses Maimonides, *Guide of the Perplexed,* trans. Shlomo Pines (Chicago: University of Chicago Press, 1963), vol. 1, p. 163]. Cohen cites the traditional Hebrew translation by Ibn Tibbon. [HW])

104.   *Quare, si Moses cum Deo de facie ad faciem, ut vir cum socio solet (hoc est mediantibus duobus corporibus) loquebatur, Christus quidem de mente ad mentem cum Deo communicavit.* (Gebhardt 3:20-21; CW 399)

105.   *Aequali jure imaginatio Prophetarum... mens Dei etiam vocari poterat, Prophetaeque mentem Dei habuisse dici poterant.* (Gebhardt 3:27; CW 403)

106.   *Nihil enim aliud significant, quam quod Prophetae virtutem singularem et supra communem habebant.* (Gebhardt 3:27; CW 403)

107.   *Et praecipue ab Hebraeis, qui se supra omnes esse jactabant, imo qui omnes, et consequenter scientiam omnibus communem, contemnare solebant.* (Gebhardt 3:27; CW 403)

108.   German: *Wissenschaft.* [RSS]

109.   *Patet deinde, cur Prophetae omnia fere parabolice, et aenigmatice perceperint, et docuerint, et omnia spiritualia corporaliter expresserint.* (Gebhardt 3:28 ; CW 404)

110.   *Nec jam mirabimur, cur Scriptura, vel Prophetae, adeo improprie, et obscure de Dei Spiritu, sive mente loquantur, ... et qui Christo aderant, Spiritum Sanctum, ut columbam descenderentem, Apostoli vero ut linguas igneas, et Paulus denique... lucem magnam viderit.* (Gebhardt 3:28-29 ; CW 404)

111.   *Qui igitur sapientiam, et rerum naturalium et spiritualium cognitionem ex Prophetarum libris investigare student, tota errant via.* (Gebhardt 3:29 ; CW 404)

112.   *Haec certitudo Prophetica mathematica quidem non erat, sed tantum moralis.* (Gebhardt 3:30; CW 405)

113.   III. *Denique, et praecipuo, quod animum ad solum aequum, et bonum inclinatum habebant.* (Gebhardt 3:31; CW 406)

114.   *Prophetiam nunquam Prophetas doctiores rededisse.* (Gebhardt 3:35; CW 409)

115.   CW 409.

116.   Cohen has modified Gebhardt's translation here to "vulgar," apparently for rhetorical effect. The Latin is "*admodum vulgares... opiniones,*" which Gebhardt rendered "sehr gewöhnliche Anschauungen," and Shirley, freely but similarly, "Their beliefs about God were shared by the vast majority of their time..." The Latin *vulgaris* means "common," "of the people," "widespread." Unlike the German *vulgär*, the Latin has no undertone of disdain, which Cohen, however, is eager to impute to Spinoza's attitude toward the prophets. [RSS]

117.   *Nihil enim singulare de divinis attributis docuerunt, vel admodum vulgares de Deo habuerunt opiniones.* (Gebhardt 3:37; CW 410)

118.   *Ob pietatem, et animi constantiam laudari, et tantopere commendari.* (Gebhardt 3:37; CW 410)

119.   *Jehova nomine, quod Hebraice haec tria tempora existendi exprimit: de ejus autem natura nihil aliud docuit, quam quod sit misericors, benignus etc. et summe zelotypus.* (Gebhardt 3:38; CW 411)

120.   Jewish tradition counts thirteen attributes of God in Exodus 34:6-7:
"merciful and gracious, long-suffering, and abundant in love and truth [*Treue*];
keeping love unto the thousandth generation, forgiving iniquity and transgression
and sin; and that will by no means clear the guilty..." [following Cohen's translation
in *Religion der Vernunft aus den Quellen des Judentums*, p. 109 = *Religion of Reason
out of the Sources of Judaism*, trans. Simon Kaplan (New York: Ungar, 1972),
p. 94]. In the last attribute, "and that will by no means clear the guilty" (ונקה לא ינקה),
traditional exegesis omits the negative particle, emphasizing the goodness of God,
and thus arrives at the modified version: "and he purifies." [Cohen's translation in
Religion der Vernunft, p. 259 = *Religion of Reason*, p. 222] In citing this passage,
Spinoza mentions neither this exegetical tradition nor the list of God's attributes,
from patience to forgiveness. [HW/RSS]

121.   *Sed quoniam Moses... nullam Dei imaginem in cerebro formaverat, ... ideo
Deus nulla ipsi imagine apparuit.* (Gebhardt 3:40; CW 412)

122.   *Concessit quidem, dari entia, quae... vicem Dei gerebant, hoc est, entia,
quibus Deus autoritatem, jus, et potentiam dedit ad dirigendas nationes, et iis
providendum et curandum; at hoc ens, quod colere tenebantur, summum et supremum
Deum, sive (ut Hebraeorum phrasi uter) Deum Deorum esse docuit.* (Gebhardt 3:39;
CW 411)

123.   I.e. the idea that Moses denies the unity and uniqueness of God. [RSS]

124.   II Chronicles 32:19. Spinoza quotes the verse without the phrase "made
by human hands." (Gebhardt 3:39; CW 411) [HW]

125.   *Docuit praeterea, hoc ens mundum hunc visibilem ex Chao... in ordinem
redegisse... et pro hoc summo suo jure, et potentia sibi soli Hebraeam nationem elegisse,
certamque mundi plagam... reliquas autem nationes, et regiones curis reliquorum
Deorum a se substitutorum reliquisse; et ideo Deus Israëlis, et Deus... Hierosolymae.*
(Gebhardt 3:39; CW 411)

126.   CW 413.

127.   *Aut quod Moses eos aliquid docuerit, quam modum vivendi, non quidem
tanquam Philosophus ut tandem ex animi libertate, sed tanquam Legis lator, ut
ex imperio Legis coacti essent bene vivere. Quare ratio bene vivendi, sive vera vita,
Deique cultus, et amor iis magiis servitus, quam vera libertas [Deique gratia et donum
fuit].* (Gebhardt 3:41; CW 413)

128.   *Nos Prophetis nihil aliud teneri credere praeter id, quod finis et substantia
est revelationis.* (Gebhardt 3:42; CW 414)

129.   CW 414.

130.   *Ad separandam Philosophiam a Theologia.* (Gebhardt 3:44; CW 415)

131.   *Societatem certis legibus formare...et omnium vires ad unum quasi corpus,
nempe societatis, redigere.* (Gebhardt 3:47; CW 418)

132.   CW 417.

133.   *Per hoc igitur tantum nationes ab invicem distinguuntur, nempe ratione societatis, et legum.* (Gebhardt 3:47; CW 418)

134.   *Adeoque Hebraea natio, non ratione intellectus, neque animi tranquillitatis a Deo prae caeteris electa fuit, sed ratione societatis, et fortunae.* (Gebhardt 3:47; CW 418)

135.   *Hebraeos in hoc solo caeteras nationes exceluisse, quod res suas, quae ad vitae securitatem pertinent, foeliciter gesserint...Dei externo auxilio, in reliquis autem caeteris aequales fuisse, et Deum omnibus aeque propitum.* (Gebhardt 3:47-48; CW 418)

136.   *At nec etiam ratione virtutis, et verae vitae.* (Gebhardt 3:48; CW 418)

137.   CW 418.

138.   *Eorum igitur electio, et vocatio in sola imperii temporanea foelicitate, et commodis constitit; nec videmus, quod Deus Patriarchis aut eorum successoribus aliud praeter hoc promiserit; imo in Lege pro obedientia nihil aliud promittur, quam imperii continua foelicitas, et reliqua hujus vitae commoda.* (Gebhardt 3:48; CW 418)

139.   Genesis 12:3.

140.   *Hoc tantum addo, Leges etiam Veteris Testamenti Judaeis tantum revelatas, et praescriptas fuisse.* (Gebhardt 3:48; CW 419)

141.   For the concept of the Noahide laws, so central to Cohen, see his essay "Die Nächstenliebe im Talmud," in *Kleinere Schriften*, vol. 2, *Jüdische Schriften*, vol. 1, p. 158ff. [HW] The essay has not been translated into English. [RSS]

142.   Cf. Gebhardt 3:49; CW 419.

143.   *Judaeos illo tempore Deo non magis dilectos fuisse, quam alias nationes... electionem Judaeorum nihil aliud spectavisse, quam temporaneam corporis foelicitatem.* (Gebhardt 3:49; CW 420)

144.   For the three passages from Psalms, see Gebhardt 3:50; CW 420.

145.   *Nam Hebraei res suas tantum, non autem aliarum gentium scribere curaverint.* (Gebhardt 3:51; CW 420)

146.   *Hebraeos prophetas non tantum suae, sed etiam multis aliis nationibus a Deo missos fuisse.* (Gebhardt 3:51)

147.   *Quare non dubium est caeteras gentes suos etiam Prophetas ut Judaeos habuisse.* (Gebhardt 3:51; CW 421)

148.   Gebhardt 3:53; CW 422.

149.   *Ridiculum sane, quod Moses praesentiam Dei gentibus invideret, aut quod tale quid a Deo ausus esset petere.* (Gebhardt 3:53)

150.   *Moses hic de sola Hebraeorum electione, ut eam explicui, [...] nec aliud a Deo petiit.* (Gebhardt 3:54; CW 423)

151.   Spinoza cites Romans 3:1-2 and 2:25-26. [HW] (Gebhardt 3:54; CW 423)

152.   *Ideo Deus omnibus nationibus Christum suum misit, qui omnes aeque a servitute legis liberaret.* (Gebhardt 3:54; CW 423)

153.   *Ne amplius ex mandato Legis, sed ex constanti animi decreto, bene agerent.* (Gerbhardt 3:54; CW 423) [Whereas Shirley renders *animus* as "heart" in CW, I have translated it as "will" in keeping with Gebhardt's German translation, "Wille," on which Cohen, in turn, bases his critique.—RSS]

154.   *Quod autem tot annos dispersi absque imperio perstiterint, id minime mirum, postquam se ab omnibus nationibus ita separaverunt, ut omnium odium in se converterint, idque non tantum ritibus externis, ...sed etiam signo circumcisionis, (quod religiosissime servant). Quod autem nationum odium eos admodum conservet, id jam experientia docuit.* (Gebhardt 3:56; CW 425)

155.   CW 425.

156.   *Signum circumcisionis etiam hac in re tantum posse existimo, ut mihi persaudeam, hoc unum hanc Nationem in aeternum conservaturum, imo nisi fundamenta suae religionis eorum animas effoeminarent, absolute crederem, eos aliquando, data occasione, ut sunt res humanae mutabiles, suum imperium iterum erecturos, Deumque eos de novo electurum.* (Gerbhardt 3:57; CW 425)

157.   Gerbhardt 3:57: *comma aliquod in capite*; cf. CW 425. [HW]

158.   CW 427.

159.   *Per humanam intelligo rationem vivendi, quae ad tutandam vitam et rempublicam tantum inservit; per divinam autem, quae solum summum bonum, hoc est, Dei veram cognitionem, et amorem spectat.* (Gebhardt 3:59; CW 427)

160.   *Cum nihil sine Deo nec esse, nec concipi posset.* (Gebhardt 3:60; CW 427)

161.   *Omnia, quae in Natura sunt, Dei conceptum... involvere, atque exprimere.* (Gebhardt 3:60; CW 428)

162.   *Quo magis res naturales cognoscimus, eo majorem, et perfectionem Dei cognotionem acquirere.* (Gebhardt 3:60; CW 428)

163.   *Summum nostrum bonum, non tantum a Dei cognitione dependet, sed in eadem omnino consistit... Media igitur... iussa Dei vocari possunt.* (Gebhardt 3:60; CW 428)

164.   *Nisi ex revelatione sanctae fuerint.* (Gebhardt 3:61; CW 429) [In CW the passage reads: "...from the latter category we must except laws that have been sanctioned by revelation." The rendition here hews more closely to the Gebhardt translation used by Cohen.—RSS]

165.   CW 428.

166.   CW 429.

167.   Ibid.

168.   *Legis igitur divinae summa, ejusque summum praeceptum est... in quo potissimum lex divina constitit [i.o. consistit]... et hoc sensu lex Mosis, quamvis non universalis, sed maxime ad ingenium et singularem conservationem unius populi accommodata fuerit, vocari tamen potest Lex Dei, sive Lex divina; quandoquidem credimus, eam lumine prophetico sancitam fuisse.* (Gebhardt 3:60-61; CW 429)

169.   Cohen reminds his reader that the *Tractatus* was published anonymously. [RSS]

170.   CW 429.

171.   *Actiones, quae in se indifferentes sunt... repraesentant... quarum ratio captum humanum superat.* (Gebhardt 3:62; CW 429) [Shirley's translation, "actions which in themselves are of no significance" (CW 429), obscures Spinoza's argument: that ceremony is morally *indifferent*, corresponding to the Stoic term *adiaphoron*.— RSS]

172.   *Summum legis divinae praemium esse, ipsam legem.* (Gebhardt 3:62; CW 429)

173.   שכר מצוה מצוה. Mishna Avot (Sayings of the Fathers) 4:2.

174.   *Deum Adamo malum tantum revelavisse, quod eum necessario sequeretur, si de illa arbore comederet, at non necessitatem consecutionis illius mali: Unde factum est, ut Adamus illam revelationem non ut aeternam et necessariam veritatem perceperit, sed ut legem, hoc est institutum, quod lucrum aut damnum sequitur.* (Gebhardt 3:63; CW 430)

175.   *Et hac etiam de causa, nempe ob defectum congitionis, Decalogus, respectu Hebraeorum tantum, lex fuit... quod si Deus nullis mediis corporeis adhibitis, sed immediate iis loquutus fuisset, hoc ipsum non tanquam legem, sed tanquam aeternam veritatem percepissent. Atque hoc, quod de Israelitis et Adamo dicimus, de onmibus etiam Prophetis... dicendum, videlicet, quod Dei decreta non adaequate, ut aeternas veritates perceperunt. Ex gr. de ipso Mose etiam dicendum est.* (Gebhardt 3:63-64; CW 431)

176.   *Non autem de Christo; de Christo enim, quamvis is etiam videatur leges Dei nomine scripsisse, sentiendum tamen est eum res vere et adaequate percepisse: nam Christus non tam Propheta, quam os Dei fuit. Deus enim per mentem Christi... quaedam humano generi revelavit.* (Gebhardt 3:64; CW 431)

177.   In German, the distinction is between the two abstract nouns *Mittelbarkeit* ("what is indirect, mediated") and *Unmittelbarkeit* ("what is direct, unmediated, without intermediary"). [RSS]

178.   *Unmittelbar*, i.e., "immediately, without intermediary." [RSS]

179.   *Et sane ex hoc, quod Deus Christo, sive ejus menti sese immediate revelaverit... nihil aliud intelligere possumus, quam quod Christus res revelatas vere percepit, sive intellexit; tum enim res intelligitur, cum ipsa pura menta extra verba et imagines percipitur.* (Gebhardt 3:64-65; CW 431)

180.   *Quare hac in vicem Dei gessit, quod sese ingenio populi accomodavit... obscure tamen, et saepius per parabolas res revelatas docuit.* (Gebhardt 3:65; CW 431f.)

181.   *Et sine dubio eos, quibus datum erat mysteria coelorum noscere, res ut aeternas veritates docuit... et hac ratione eos a servitute legis liberavit, et nihilominus legem hoc magis confirmavit et stabilivit.* (Gebhardt 3:65; CW 432)

182.   *Quae omnia cum scientia naturali plane conveniunt; haec enim Ethicam docet, et veram virtutem.* (Gebhardt 3:68; CW 434) ["Excellence of knowledge" is a rendering of "scientiae praestantia," for which Shirley has the less accurate "the excellence of understanding."—RSS]

183.   *In quinque... libris, qui Mosis vulgo dicuntur...* (Gebhardt 3:70; CW 436) [Shirley's translation is more accurate than Cohen's Gebhardt edition, "...mit den 'sogenannten fünf Büchern Mose'" ("the so-called five books of Moses").—RSS]

184.   The phrase "that have regard only for the utility of the commonwealth" ("et quae adeo etiam solius imperii utilitatem spectant") is lacking(!) in Shirley's translation. [RSS]

185.   *Et quamvis quinque illi libri, praeter ceremonias, multa moralia contineant, haec tamen in iis non continentur, tanquam documenta moralia, onmibus hominibus universalia, sed tanquam mandata... Ex gr. Moses non tanquam doctor aut Propheta Judaeos docet, ne occidant neque furentur, sed haec tanquam legislator et princeps jubet; non enim documenta ratione comprobat, sed jussibus poenam addit... Sic etiam iussum de non comittendo adulterio solius, reipublicae et imperii utilitatem respicit; nam si documentum morale docere voluisset... tum non tantum actionem externam, sed et ipsum animi consensum damnaret.* (Gebhardt 3:70; CW 436)

186.   See also p. 58.

187.   Cf. "Der Sabbath in seiner culturgeschichtlichen Bedeutung" ("The Sabbath in Its Cultural-Historical Significance"), *Kleinere Schriften*, vol. 1, *Jüdische Schriften*, vol. 2, pp. 45-72. [HW]

188.   *Quasi diceret, Deum post urbis vastationem nihil singulare a Judaeis exigere, nec aliud ab iisdem in posterum petere praeter legem naturalem.* (Gebhardt 3:72; CW 437)

189.   CW 437.

190.   *...caeremonias autem... missas fecerunt Apostoli.* The translation follows

Gebhardt. Shirley's is looser: "while the Apostles made no mention of ceremonial rites." (CW 437) [RSS]

191.   *Quod autem Pharisaei... aut saltem magnam earum partem retinuerint, id magis animo Christianis adversandi, quam Deo placendi fecerunt.* (Gebhardt 3:72; CW 437)

192.   *Nam post primam urbis vastationem... statim ceremonias neglexerunt, imo toti legi Mosis valedixerunt.* (Gebhardt 3:72; CW 437)

193.   CW 440.

194.   Cohen refers here to p. 105 of the Gebhardt translation, which corresponds roughly to pp. 441-442 in Shirley, and in which I was unable to locate a phrase similar to "constant thought." (CW 441f.)

195.   *Se nihil prorsus sui, sed omnino alterius juris esse: ex quibus omnibus luce clarius constat, caeremonias ad beatitudinem nihil facere, et illas Veteris Testamenti, imo totam legem Mosis nihil aliud, quam Hebraeorum imperium, et consequenter nihil praeter corporis commoda spectavisse.* (Gebhardt 3:76; CW 440) [Shirley inexplicably reads *corporis commoda* as "temporal prosperity" instead of "physical advantages."—RSS]

196.   Gebhardt's translation reads that they "nur unter fremdem Rechte ständen" ("omnino alterius juris esse").

197.   *Quod autem ad Christianorum ceremonias attinet, nempe Baptismum, Coenam dominicam, festa, orationes externas... si eae unquam a Christo, aut ab Apostolis institutae sunt (quod adhuc mihi non satis constat), eae nonnisi ut universalis Ecclesiae signa externa institutae sunt, non autem ut res... quae aliquid Sanctimoniae in se habeant.* (Gebhardt 3:76; CW 440)

198.   Henry Oldenburg (d. 1678) was the secretary of the Royal Society in London from 1664 on and had known Spinoza since 1661. Their correspondence ended at the beginning of 1676, because of differences of opinion on the theological interpretation of the resurrection of Christ, *inter alia*. Cf. Spinoza's letters 78 and 79. (CW 952-954) [HW]

199.   The Swiss Protestant theologian Huldrych Zwingli (1484-1531), whose view, for example, on the Last Supper shifted attention from transubstantiation to the transformation of the participants in the Eucharist. [RSS]

200.   *Hujus rei exemplum in regno Japonensium habetur, ubi Christiana religio interdicta est, et Belgae, qui ibi habitant, ex mandato Societatis Indiae Orientalis ab omni externo cultu abstinere tenentur.* (Gebhardt 3:76; CW 440)

201.   CW 442.

202.   *Vulgus [...] eas tantum historias, quae maxime eorum animos ad obediantiam et devotionem movere possunt, scire tenetur.* (Gebhardt 3:79; CW 442)

203. *Quare si quis historias S. Scripturae legerit, eisque [i.o. eique] in omnibus fidem habuerit, nec tamen ad doctrinam, quam ipsa iisdem docere intendit, attenderit, nec vitam emendaverit, perinde ipsi est, ac si Alcoranum, aut Poëtarum fabulas Scenicas, aut saltem communia chronica ea attentione, qua vulgus solet, legisset.* (Gebhardt 3:79; CW 442f)

204. Cohen, presumably citing from memory, added the words "for you." [RSS]

205. Cf. Sanhedrin 56a. [HW]

206. J. Selden, *De iure naturali et gentium iuxta disciplinam Ebraeorum* (1665). In *Religion der Vernunft*, p. 143 (= *Religion of Reason*, p. 123f.), Cohen mentions an edition published in "London 1640." The following citations are from *Johannis Selden juris consulti Opera omnia tam edita tam inedita*, ed. David Wilkins (London, 1726), vol. 1, p. 66, col. 757. On his estimation of the Noahide, cf. bk. I, praefatio, p. 68f.; cap. 8, col. 147; and, above all, cap. 10, col. 158ff. [HW]

207. *At Judaei contra plane sentiunt, statuunt enim, veras opiniones, veramque vivendi rationem nihil prodesse ad beatitudinem, quamdiu homines eas ex solo lumine naturali amplectuntur et non ut documenta Mosi prophetice revelata: hoc enim Maimonides... aperte his verbis audet affirmare. Maimon. c. 8. Regum lege 11.* (CW 443) [Maimonides, *Mishneh Torah*, Laws of Kings 8:11—RSS]

208. Cohen translates here—as in his quotations from the Bible—directly from the Hebrew, unlike Gebhardt, who translates from Spinoza's Latin version. [HW]

209. Cf. "Liebe und Gerechtigkeit in den Begriffen Gott und Mensch," *Kleinere Schriften*, vol. 3, *Jüdische Schriften*, vol. 3, p. 60. [HW]

210. הגוים לא מעלין ולא מורידין ויש לחסידין חלק לעולם הבא. ("The other nations we neither exalt nor demean, and the pious among them have a share in eternal life").

211. Manuel Joël, *Spinozas Theologisch-politischer Traktat, auf seine Quellen geprüft*, p. 56; reprinted in *Beiträge zur Geschichte der Philosophie*, vol. 2 (Breslau: Skutsch, 1876). [Here the text of an annotation should be included—cf. also *Jüdische Schriften*— that was appended in the *Jahrbuch für jüdische Geschichte*, without being assigned to any specific passage.] Furthermore, Joël pointed out that the correct reading is to be found in a booklet encompassing only twenty-four pages in quarto, *Kebod Elohim*. Spinoza cites it here as confirmation of Maimonides' view, thus proving that the fact was not unknown to him, that Maimonides, in this instance, is in no way representative of rabbinic doctrine. For this reason, he draws on a book lacking any authority.

212. Cf. Joël, *Theologisch-politischer Traktat*, p. 56: according to *Kebod Elohim* (cf. Cohen's annotation) the final words of Maimonides in Laws of Kings 8:11 read: אבל מחכמיהם, and thus not ולא מחכ' or ואינו מחכ', as in Spinoza (the *editio princeps* and those editions that follow it read ולא מחכ' and, if they have an apparatus of variant readings, list אלא מחכמ', supporting Joël's position, and conforming with

the manuscript in the Oxford Bodleian Library, *inter alia*). In Cohen's translation the last sentence would then read: "But he who observes them [the Noahide commandments] only through a decision of his reason is not a resident sojourner and [...] belongs not to the pious of the nations of the world, *but* to their sages." The author of *Kebod Elohim* is Joseph ben Shemtov, whom Spinoza quotes immediately after the contested citation from Maimonides. (Gebhardt 3:79; CW 443) According to Joël, Spinoza intentionally overlooked ben Shemtov's reading with its qualifying "but," to the detriment of Maimonides (p. 56). [HW]

213.   Cf. the well-known commentary כסף משנה by Joseph Karo ad loc.: Maimonides' opinion proceeds from his own thinking (מסברא דנפשיה). However, Cohen does not indicate that this commentary concurs with Maimonides' thinking, for the commentary continues: "and [his opinion] is the correct one" (ונכוחה היא). Cohen's preferred reading is documented neither in this commentary nor in any other traditional commentary, as would be necessary, and contrary to his claim in the last sentence of the preceding paragraph. [HW]

214.   Van Vloten and Land 2:21 ad loc. [N.B. Cohen is referring to J. van Vloten and J.P. N. Land, the editors of the then current Latin edition of Spinoza's works, *Benedicti de Spinoza Opera*, 2nd ed. (The Hague: Martin Nijhoff, 1895)—RSS] The note refers to the variant readings mentioned above and selects the variant אלא מחכ' as the best. "Suppl. p. 146" refers not to Van Vloten and Land, but to Cohen's note inserted above (after "Joël"). [HW]

215.   Cohen is now referring to Maimonides. [RSS]

216.   Cohen is referring to the debate regarding whether all non-Jews are condemned to the netherworld (R. Eliezer) or only some of them (R. Joshua). The concept of the Noahide turns the debate in R. Joshua's favor. [HW]

217.   Cohen: *Beisaßfremdling*, referring to גר תושב. [RSS]

218.   Laws of Kings 8:10: "He who recognizes them [the Noahide commandments] is called a resident sojourner." (המקבל אותם הוא הנקרא גר תושב בכל מקום) [HW]

219.   *Hilchot Teshuva.*

220.   *Hilchot Edut.*

221.   The "Maimonidean annotations/emendations" (הגהות מיימוניות) contain nothing on this passage (*Regum lege* 8:10). However, the commentary mentioned above, כסף משנה, cites, in connection with the last sentence in this section (וכל המקבל עליו וכו'), a remark by R. Yohanan beginning with the assumption that a resident sojourner (גר תושב) is the subject under discussion. [HW]

222.   *Eam fixum atque immutabilem ordinem servare; ... legesque naturae adeo perfectas et fertiles esse, ut iis nihil addi neque detrahi possit... sequitur, miracula res naturales fuisse.* (Gebhardt 3:96; CW 455)

223. *Methodum interpretandi Scripturam haud differre a methodo interpretandi naturam, sed cum ea prorsus convenire.* (Gebhardt 3:98; CW 457)

224. CW 457.

225. *Nam sicuti methodus interpretandi naturam in hoc potissimum consistit, in concinnanda scilicet historia naturae, ex qua, utpote ex certis datis, rerum naturalium definitiones concludimus: sic etiam ad Scripturam interpretandam necesse est ejus sinceram historiam adornare, et ex ea tanquam ex certis datis et principiis mentem authorum Scripturae legitimis consequentiis concludere... Quare cognitio horum omnium... ab ipsa Scriptura sola peti debet: sicuti cognitio naturae ab ipsa natura. Quod ad documenta moralia, ... attinet, etsi ipsa ex notionibus communibus demonstrari possunt, non potest tamen ex iisdem demonstrari, Scripturam eadem docere, sed hoc ex sola ipsa Scriptura constare postest.* (Gebhardt 3:98-99; CW 457)

226. "Hebraizant tamen." (Gebhardt 3:100; CW 458) Shirley translates: "their idiom is Hebraic." [RSS]

227. CW 458.

228. *Quamdiu sensum Scripturae quaerimus, ne ratiocinio nostro... praeoccupemur; sed... ille ex solo linguae usu erit investigandus... quod Deus sit ignis, et quod Deus sit zelotypus, quam clarissimae sunt, quamdiu ad solam verborum significationem attendimus... tametsi respectu veritatis et rationis obscurrissimae sunt.* (Gebhardt 3:100; CW 459)

229. *Haec et similia Scriptura ex professo, et tanquam aeternam doctrinam non docet.* (Gebhardt 3:100; CW 460)

230. *At mundi aeternitas nulla demonstratione ostenditur; adeoque non est necesse Scripturis vim facere.* (Gebhardt 3:114; CW 468) [In the original, Spinoza quotes from the Ibn Tibbon Hebrew version of the *Guide of the Perplexed* (2:25) and translates it into Latin.—RSS]

231. "Lumen naturale" (cf. Gebhardt 3:114f.). The term is used often in this passage, but without the modifying "common." [HW]

232. The original text reads: "philosophantum," which, accurately translated, means not "of philosophy," but "of philosophers." Cf. the next note and CW 469. [RSS]

233. *Vulgus... de Scriptura nihil nisi ex sola authoritate et testimoniis philosophorum [i.o. philosophantum] admittere poterit... quae sane nova esset Ecclesiae authoritas, novumque sacerdotum vel Pontificum genus.* (Gebhardt 3:114; CW 469) [I have made minor adjustments in the English translation in CW.—RSS]

234. CW 471.

235. Latin: the "common people." [RSS]

236. *Hoc certo affirmare possum, me nullam animadvertisse mendam, nec*

lectionum varietatem, circa moralia documenta, quae ipsa obscura aut dubia reddere possent. (Gebhardt 3:135; CW 485)

237.   *Nam hi non vocati sunt, ut omnibus nationibus praedicarent et prophetarent, sed quibusdam tantum peculiaribus.* (Gebhardt 3:154; CW 501)

238.   *Cum itaque statuendum sit, Epistolas Apostolorum a solo Lumine Naturali dictatas fuisse.* (Gebhardt 3:155)

239.   CW 502. The translation has been modified to match Gebhardt's German edition. [RSS]

240.   *Deinde, quamvis religio, prout ab Apostolis praedicabantur, nempe simplicem Christi historiam narrando, sub Rationem non cadat, eius tamen summam, quae potissimum documentis moralibus constat, ut tota Christi doctrina, potest unusquisque lumine naturali facile assequi.* (Gebhardt 3:156; CW 502)

241.   Matthew 5ff. See "Supplementary Note 27" in CW 580; Gebhardt 3:262. [HW/RSS]

242.   The full title of chapter 12 is "Of the true Original of the Divine Law. In what respect Scripture is called holy and the Word of God. It is shown that Scripture, insofar as it contains the Word of God, has come down to us uncorrupted." (CW 503) [RSS]

243.   *Tanquam legem catholicam, et ex sola vi passionis Christi omnibus praedicaverunt Apostoli.* (Gebhardt 3:163; CW 507)

244.   *At no quod doctrina diversi sint... nec denique quod religio catholica, quae maxime naturalis est, nova esset, nisi respectu hominum, qui eam non noverant.* (Gebhardt 3:163; CW 507)

245.   *Documentum charitatis, quae ubique in utroque testamento summe commendatur.* (Gebhardt 3:164; CW 509) [Cohen, following Gebhardt, translates *charitas* as "Liebe" ("love"). Shirley (CW) has "charity."—RSS]

246.   CW 540.

247.   CW 547.

248.   Cohen refers to parts 3 and 4 of the *Ethics*, on the nature of the emotions (*affectus*). The basis of the discussion is Spinoza's definition of hatred as "pain accompanied by the idea of an external cause." (bk. 3, prop. 13, schol.; CW 286) [RSS]

249.   *Nam cives nullibi maiore iure bona sua possidebant, quam huius imperii subditi, qui cum principe aequalem partem terrarum et agrorum habebant, et unusquisque suae partis aeternus dominus erat.* (Gebhardt 3:202; CW 547)

250.   CW 547.

251.   *Quam periculosum sit ad ius divinum referre res mere speculativas.* (Gebhardt 3:225; CW 555)

252. *Et ideo iis dictum fuit: dilige proximum tuum, odio habe inimicum tuum.* (Gebhardt 3:233; CW 561)

253. The original reads *"innerliche* Bibelforschung," literally, "internal study of the Bible." [RSS]

254. *Quae omnia evidentissime ostendunt, religionem reipublicae utilitati accomodatam semper fuisse.* (Gebhardt 3:233; CW 561)

255. "Discipline" is used here in the ecclesiastical sense of a system of rules and procedures by which order is maintained in a religious group. [RSS]

256. "Das Kleinod der Kirche ist der Bann." According to Jakob Freudenthal, *Spinoza, sein Leben und seine Lehre*, vol. 1, *Das Leben Spinozas* (Stuttgart: Fr. Frommann, 1904), this was the opinion of Menno Simons, the founder of the "Mennonites" (p. 76). Spinoza is said to have been close to them as well as to the "Collegiants" ("Rhynsburgians") (pp. 65ff.).

257. German: "Stamm."

258. Cf. Spinoza's letter no. 73 to Oldenburg, cited above in Cohen's annotation, n. 102. [HW]

259. Cohen is alluding to the circumstances of Mendelssohn's death. Exhausted by his efforts to defend Lessing against Jacobi's posthumous charge of Spinozism, Mendelssohn contracted a fatal chill while delivering his manuscript "To the Friends of Lessing" to his publisher on a frosty winter day. Cf. Alexander Altmann, *Moses Mendelssohn: A Biographical Study* (London: Routledge & Kegan Paul, 1973), pp. 739-741. [RSS]

260. Cf. "Über die Lehre des Spinoza in Briefen an Herrn Moses Mendelssohn," in *Jacobi's Werke* (Leipzig: Gerhard Fleischer, 1812-1815), vol. 4.1, p. 55, where Lessing is produced as a witness that "there is no philosophy other than the philosophy of Spinoza." [HW]

261. Cf. Kant's position on the controversy between Mendelssohn and Jacobi in his essay "Was heißt, sich im Denken orientieren?" *Kant Akademie-Ausgabe*, vol. 8, p. 134. [HW] See also Altmann's summary of Kant's position in *Moses Mendelssohn*, pp. 750-753. [RSS]

262. An allusion to the title of Kant's late treatise on religion, *Religion innerhalb der Grenzen der bloßen Vernunft* (1793-1794) ("Religion Within the Limits of Reason Alone"). [RSS]

263. Cf. Friedrich Daniel Ernst Schleiermacher, *On Religion: Speeches to Its Cultured Despisers*, trans. Richard Crouter on the basis of the original 1799 edition (Cambridge and New York: Cambridge University Press, 1996), p. 24: "Respectfully offer up with me a lock of hair to the manes of the holy rejected Spinoza! The high world spirit permeated him, the infinite was his beginning and end, the universe his only and eternal love; in holy innocence and deep humility he was reflected in the

eternal world and saw how he too was its most lovable mirror; he was full of religion and full of holy spirit..." In later editions, Schleiermacher restrained his pathos and distanced himself from Spinoza's "system." [HW/RSS]

264.   Cf. Strauss, *Leben Jesu* (*Life of Jesus*, 1835-36).

265.   I.e., the *Theological-Political Treatise*. [RSS]

266.   On Heine's "Jewish anguish" (*Judenschmerz*), cf. his letter to Moses Moser of June 18, 1823: "I feel a great urge to express my great Jewish anguish (as Börne calls it) in an essay for the *Zeitschrift [für die Wissenschaft des Judentums]*. Was the old baron of Sinai and monarch of Judea likewise enlightened, dispensing with his nationality, forfeiting his claims and his followers, in favor of a few vague, cosmopolitan ideas? I fear the old gentleman lost his head, and *le petit juif d'Amsterdam* [the little Jew of Amsterdam] may rightly whisper in his ear: *entre nous, Monsieur, vous n'existez pas* [Just between us, Sir, you do not exist]" (Heinrich Heine, *Säkularausgabe, Werke, Briefwechsel, Lebenszeugnisse*, vol. 20, *Briefe 1815-1831* [Berlin: Akademieverlag, 1970], p. 97). See also Hermann Cohen's essay "Heinrich Heine und das Judentum," in *Kleinere Schriften*, vol. 1, *Jüdische Schriften*, vol. 2, pp. 34f. [HW]

267.   I.e. in anti-Semitic political camps. [RSS]

268.   Freudenthal, *Das Leben Spinozas*, p. 166.

269.   Ibid., p. 167.

270.   Ibid.

271.   Ibid., p. 168.

272.   Ibid., p. 170.

273.   Ibid., p. 171.

274.   Ibid., p. 172.

275.   Ibid., p. 175.

276.   Ibid., p. 176.

277.   Ibid., p. 177.

278.   Ibid., p. 178.

279.   Ibid.

280.   Ibid.

281.   Ibid.

282.   Ibid., p. 179.

283.   Jean Bodin, *Colloquium Heptaplomeres, De Rerum sublimium arcanis*

abditis, ed. Ludwig Noack (Schwerin: Fr. W. Bärensprung, 1857) (written before 1593). In this fictitious dialogue between representatives of various religious faiths, Bodin's sympathy lies mainly with Judaism. [HW]

284. Freudenthal, *Das Leben Spinozas*, p. 197.

285. Ibid.

286. Ibid., p. 198.

287. Ibid., pp. 199f.

288. "Ethnic compatriots" is a rendering of *Stammesgenossen*. [RSS]

289. Freudenthal, *Das Leben Spinozas*, pp. 200f.

290. Ibid., p. 201.

291. I.e., the view presented by Freudenthal in his Spinoza biography. [RSS]

292. Freudenthal, *Das Leben Spinozas*, p. 201.

293. Ibid.

294. Ibid., p. 420.

295. Ibid.

296. Cohen cites two painters of everyday life in Holland, Jan Steen (ca. 1626-1679) and Adriaen van Ostade (1610-1685), as contrasts to Spinoza's contempt toward common people and the peasantry. [RSS]

297. "Members of his people or nation" is a rendering of *Volks- und Stammesgenossen*. [RSS]

298. Freudenthal, *Das Leben Spinozas*, pp. 202f.

299. Ibid., p. 244.

300. Ibid., p. 217.

301. See, for example, the second-to-last paragraph of Spinoza's preface to the *Theological-Political Treatise*. (CW 393-394) [HW]

302. Cf. speech 11 in Fichte, *Reden an die deutsche Nation*, the passage on the "class [of the nation] that is actually the basis of humankind" and the education of which should be the most pressing goal of national education, *Sämmtliche Werke*, edited by I.H. Fichte (Berlin: Veit und Co., 1845-46), vol. 7, p. 430. [HW]

303. German: *wissenschaftlicher Idealismus*, where *wissenschaftlich* may mean "scientific," "systematic," or "academic." [RSS]

304. Cf. Julius Guttmann, "Kant und das Judentum," in *Zwei Vorträge, gehalten in der Generalversammlung der Gesellschaft für die Wissenschaft des Judentums*

am 23.12.1907 zu Berlin (Berlin and Leipzig: Gustav Fock, 1908), pp. 50f. [There, Guttmann reports on the far-reaching effect of the presentation of Judaism in the *Theological-Political Treatise*, a product of "passionate hatred." According to him, Kant also followed this widespread conception.—HW]

INDEX